OTHER PEOPLE'S MOTHERS

UNIVERSITY PRESS OF FLORIDA

Florida A&M University, Tallahassee
Florida Atlantic University, Boca Raton
Florida Gulf Coast University, Ft. Myers
Florida International University, Miami
Florida State University, Tallahassee
New College of Florida, Sarasota
University of Central Florida, Orlando
University of Florida, Gainesville
University of North Florida, Jacksonville
University of South Florida, Tampa
University of West Florida, Pensacola

Other People's Mothers

Julie Marie Wade

UNIVERSITY PRESS OF FLORIDA

Gainesville
Tallahassee
Tampa
Boca Raton
Pensacola
Orlando
Miami
Jacksonville
Ft. Myers
Sarasota

30 29 28 27 26 25   6 5 4 3 2 1

Library of Congress Cataloging-in-Publication Data
Names: Wade, Julie Marie, author.
Title: Other people's mothers / Julie Marie Wade.
Description: Gainesville : University Press of Florida, [2025]
Identifiers: LCCN 2025004302 (print) | LCCN 2025004303 (ebook) |
    ISBN 9780813081144 (paperback) | ISBN 9780813073927 (ebook)
Subjects: LCSH: Mothers and daughters. | Mothers.
Classification: LCC HQ755.85 .W33 2025 (print) | LCC HQ755.85 (ebook) |
    DDC 306.874/3—dc23/eng/20250221
LC record available at https://lccn.loc.gov/2025004302
LC ebook record available at https://lccn.loc.gov/2025004303

The University Press of Florida is the scholarly publishing agency for the State University
System of Florida, comprising Florida A&M University, Florida Atlantic University, Florida
Gulf Coast University, Florida International University, Florida State University, New College
of Florida, University of Central Florida, University of Florida, University of North Florida,
University of South Florida, and University of West Florida.

University Press of Florida
2046 NE Waldo Road
Suite 2100
Gainesville, FL 32609
http://upress.ufl.edu

GPSR EU Authorized Representative: Mare Nostrum Group B.V., Mauritskade 21D,
1091 GC Amsterdam, The Netherlands, gpsr@mare-nostrum.co.uk

For all the mothers who weren't mine

—& the one mother who was

Never to be someone's mother, no.
But someone's friend
—someone's mother's friend
to whom two girls, late and soaked through,
come home:
to the two of us at the table, drinking.
How is it
I'm no longer one of them, running in from the rain, but
someone's friend's mother's friend

—JAMESON FITZPATRICK, "SMALL ACTORS"

CONTENTS

CONTENTS

Mrs. Mann

[Or a Study of the Fates of Different Drummers]

Steven Mann was the closest I ever came to having a brother, if you don't count the imaginary ones. He might also qualify as my first sweetheart, which sounds a little incestuous I know, but we were six at the time, then seven, and the lines between the different kinds of love were blurry at best—though perhaps they always are.

We met in kindergarten when Steven transferred to West Seattle Christian from a Montessori school. He was the kid who wore jeans patterned like speckled eggs and had bright yellow hair cut in the shape of a bowl. I liked him instantly, in part because he didn't know the routine and needed me to lead him around. Our mothers seemed to like each other, too, and stood chatting and chatting at pickup time, so eventually I got to ride along in the Mann Mobile—the wood-paneled minivan that Steven's mother drove—while my own mother came to their house to retrieve me later on.

When I think of it now, Mrs. Mann and my mom had a lot in common. They were both women who, in a vocabulary I did not yet possess, might be described as "overly concerned with appearances." Mrs. Mann, for instance, always wore slacks with unnatural creases, as if she had spent hours bent over an ironing board, and blouses that buttoned all the way to her chin. My mother favored brighter prints, taller shoes, and shoulder pads more mountain than molehill, but she, too, spent a lot of time smoothing wrinkles and rolling away lint.

Another word that comes to mind is "provincial." Both mothers were frightened to the point of panic that the world around them had veered suddenly off course, as indicated by phrases like "to hell in a handcart" and "a few rotten apples can spoil the whole barrel." Such maxims had something to do with Madonna and Michael Jackson and several other "oversexed celebrities," but thankfully, they had Ronald Reagan in the White House, and he was the man they hoped would turn it all around.

When we burst through the door, the Mann house was always immaculate, redolent of cleaning products and potpourri, which I once accidentally ate before Steven explained what it was.

"My mom puts it out so we can't smell the litter box," he said, hands on his hips to convey an air of authority.

"Why doesn't your cat go to the bathroom outside?" My mother insisted I must never say "poop" or "pee," as these descriptions were characteristic of low-class people and children who were raised by wolves.

"She doesn't have claws, so if we let her out in the backyard, she couldn't defend herself and would be eaten to death by raccoons."

"Oh." I nodded at first. "But why doesn't she have claws?"

Steven explained that if she had claws, she would climb the drapes and tear up the furniture. Children weren't even allowed to sit on the couch in the Mann family living room, but this clawless kitty—whose name was Amanda and who had gray tiger stripes and dainty white feet—could sleep there undisturbed on a pillow all day.

Johnny, the basset hound, reliably lolled on a rug at her feet, paws over his nose and eyes closed. Occasionally, he raised his droopy lids and howled.

"How come all your animals have people names?" I asked, following Steven down the carpeted stairs to the playroom. He shrugged and didn't answer. For a long quiet time, we sat cross-legged on the floor with an unfinished Jenga tower between us. Finally, he said, not looking at me, "You know what I wish? I wish we could trade in my brother for a parakeet. *Ryan* would be the perfect name for a parakeet."

Steven's brother Ryan had something my mother called "hyper-activity" when she and my father discussed the Manns over dinner at home. Ryan was two years younger than Steven and described by most adults as "bouncing off the walls," which was why he had to take medicine and spend a lot of time in Time Out. Ryan was a shorter, faster, louder version of Steven, with hair the same daf-fodil color and cut in the same soup-bowl style. He played tee ball and soccer and took karate lessons, but none of these activities seemed to calm him down. Even then, we could hear him clamber-ing around the house, his little feet less a pitter-patter than a series of short, hard thuds.

"So, do you play any sports?" I asked Steven. This moment marked my emerging understanding that sometimes, by asking a question you already know the answer to, you can move the con-versation along toward a harder question, the kind a mother might censor by calling you "impudent," then make you apologize.

"No," he said, "I play piano." Proudly then, he sprang to his feet and strode across the room to the baby grand. Steven lifted the shiny black lid and positioned it on a stick that held the whole piano open, spread wide like an elephant ear so all the wires inside were showing.

I perched on the bench beside him, listening as he explained how his mother believed he could be a prodigy if he just kept working at it, and he must have been getting really close because he had been working at it already for close to three years. I watched his chubby fingers travel the white keys like a highway, the black keys set apart for special occasions. Below us, one of his sneakered feet worked the damper pedal, which made the notes blur and the sound carry on long after Steven had finished striking the keys.

There was a funny brown box beside the sheet music on the shelf, and as soon as my eyes settled on it, Steven opened the box and set the strange silver clock to ticking. "It helps you keep time," he explained, and by then, for some reason, I had forgotten the harder question I wanted to ask before. Instead, I leaned over and kissed him. He kept playing, as if he expected my soft mouth on his pink cheek all along.

"What do you think about piano lessons, Julie?" my mother asked one night while plunging her hands into soapy water. My father was sweeping the kitchen floor, and I held a damp towel in my hand, waiting for the next dish to dry.

"I think I'm a little young yet," I replied.

"Mrs. Mann says Steven started when he was only three years old."

"What's a boy doing playing piano anyway?" my father asked.

"It helps with coordination and penmanship," my mother retorted with a splash. "And besides, not every girl wants to end up with an uncultured Neanderthal."

My father's laugh had a nervous tinge, so he tickled me to lighten the mood.

"Just the same," I said, "I already have ballet and swimming lessons." I was also scheduled to start track with the West Seattle Striders in the fall.

"Kids have to have some free time," my father concurred, handing me the dustpan. "Too many lessons and you defeat the whole purpose of being a kid."

Squatting down, I watched the gray clouds of dust tangled with crumbs that my father brushed toward me. Behind my back, I crossed one set of fingers so tight they began to tingle by the time I released them.

All at once, it's first grade, and we move to the bigger classroom near the bigger playground, and it doesn't matter that Steven is almost a prodigy at piano because he is bad at kickball, and everyone—boys and girls alike—makes fun of him for tripping over his untied shoes.

Everyone, that is, except me. "I wish I had Velcro ones," Steven laments, "but my mom won't let me get Velcro. She says they cost more and make you lazy."

"My mom says the same thing," I sigh, "and I have to wear loafers because I'm a girl."

"That's stupid. Lots of girls wear tennis shoes."

This I know, but my mother believes tennis shoes are for home and not school, no exception. She faults them for not being "lady-like" and warns me I must never, ever wear them with a dress. My mother even wears heels with her jeans, and jeans only on the rarest occasions.

"Girls are lucky, though," Steven murmurs after a while, wiping his eyes on his sleeve. "They can wear pants sometimes and dresses sometimes, but boys can *never* wear dresses. Not even once. Not even for Halloween."

As we sit together on the crumbling curb beside the cyclone fence at recess—despite the fact that I am good at kickball and itching to play—Steven explains how he saw a picture of Florence Nightingale in our *Weekly Reader* and wanted to go as her for Halloween. "It's a simple dress," he pouts, "and I know my mother could make it on her sewing machine." There is also a hat that looks like a doily, and we both live in homes with doilies galore. "It wouldn't cost a thing for me to go as Florence Nightingale, and then I could carry that creaky old lamp."

On a whim: "What's your brother going as?"

"A zombie skeleton," Steven groans, his head drooping like a dandelion over clean, stonewashed knees. "My dad took him to the store and bought him this whole glow-in-the-dark outfit. Now my dad's trying to make me go as He-Man or Skeletor."

"Do you have a second choice?" I ask, keeping one eye on the game and one eye on Steven.

He blows through his plump, pink lips, making a motorboat sound. "The only one that even comes close is Betsy Ross," and we both understand implicitly that a flag is no match for a lamp.

Recently, I have taken to bringing my collection of My Little Ponies over to Steven's house where we are building stables out of Jenga pieces in his backyard. We are also devising a new game where the ponies become possessed by demons and swell in size, at which point we usurp their identities and run around cursing other creatures in the barnyard, which sometimes include Steven's cat, dog, and brother.

"Let's go as My Little Ponies for Halloween," I suggest, as we lie panting on the carpet in our soiled clothes.

"The regular ones or the demon-possessed?"

"Demon-possessed!" I exclaim happily, then look up to find Mrs. Mann standing on the landing, a can of Comet in one hand and a Brillo pad in the other.

"I'm not sure I want to speculate about the conversation taking place down here," she begins in a low, unsettling tone. "Steven, what have I told you about traipsing around the house in your dirty tennis shoes?"

"Oh." His white face drinks up shame like a red carnation. "We were supposed to leave them on the back porch."

"And what happened to your pants? Why are they covered in mud?"

"That was my fault," I offer. "We were playing My Little Ponies, and I turned on the hose to make the leaves slick and mushy. Better for sliding."

Mrs. Mann leaves the room abruptly, and we scramble to remove our shoes. When she returns, she hands Steven a bottle of Resolve and instructs him to clean the carpets where we have "fouled" them. I don't like the sound of this word or the expression on Mrs. Mann's face as she says it. For the rest of the visit, we are relegated to the garage where we sit on orange crates—clammy now, with our shoulders hunched and our teeth chattering—and plan our spectacular Halloween.

At home, my mother sends my father to give me a "good talking-to." She says I don't take her authority seriously because she is only a woman, and I want to protest that the scariest people I know are women, my mom and Mrs. Mann foremost among them. Wisely, though, I say nothing. My father, who is gentle and soft-spoken and hasn't been around much until recently—due to his traveling salesman job that I like to pretend is actually espionage—taps lightly on my bedroom door after dinner. This is how I know it's my father. If it were my mother, she would just barge right in.

"Hey, Smidge," he says, "are you all cleaned up now?"

I look down at my pink-and-white-striped pajamas and nod. He is doing it, too—asking a question he already knows the answer to—probably as a warm-up for a harder question.

"Good. So, before we read our Nancy Drew tonight, I thought we could talk a little about you and Steven Mann."

Lately, everyone wants to talk to me about Steven Mann, the kids who think he's "weird" and the teachers who think he's "troubled." Defensive already, I blurt out, "Steven wants to go as Florence Nightingale for Halloween, and I think his mother should let him!"

"But Florence Nightingale is a woman."

"So what? She's *historical!*"

"There are other historical figures," my father says, sitting down beside me on the bed and patting my knee. "Steven could go as Paul Revere or George Washington. What about Abraham Lincoln with a nice tall hat?"

"He wants the lamp, Dad. Florence Nightingale was the Lady with the Lamp."

"Look, Julie, whatever Steven Mann goes as for Halloween—that's up to his parents. But we've been hearing some alarming things from Mrs. Mann about your behavior. She says you kids are rambunctious and disobedient. You've been making a mess in her yard and tracking mud through her house and doing some disturbing things with the My Little Ponies we bought you."

"We're just playing, Dad."

"Well, let's try to be a little bit more ladylike, shall we? You're a girl, and you should be a good influence on Steven, show him what being clean and respectful means."

"Why does everyone keep telling me I'm a girl?" I retort. "I *know* I'm a girl." Folding my arms across my chest, I stare at the white wicker vanity with the pink-cushioned chair and, channeling Steven, refuse to meet my father's eyes.

"Listen, Smidge," he says, his voice still steady and calm, "*you* could go as Florence Nightingale."

"I don't want to be some stupid nurse. I want to be a sleuth like Nancy Drew."

"So maybe—you go as Nancy Drew and Steven could go as Ned Nickerson. What about that?"

It isn't a terrible idea, but I have a feeling Steven will want to be Bess.

When I see Steven at school the next day, he tells me that we aren't allowed to play My Little Ponies anymore and that he might not be coming to the annual costume party.

"My mother says you're a bad influence and that I have to branch out and try to make new friends."

"Don't worry," I reassure him. "Lots of people's mothers have said I'm a bad influence, but then they just forget about it and have another baby."

Steven tugs the zipper on his windbreaker up and down, and I can tell he is thinking about Florence Nightingale. "Let's be really good and help your mom sort the laundry, and then she'll like us again, and you can go to the party. Maybe we should go as Nancy Drew and Ned Nickerson."

"I don't even know who they are," he sighs, turning away and wiping his nose on his sleeve so I won't see he's crying.

"Only the most famous girl-detective ever and her boyfriend!" I proclaim, watching as the other kids split into two teams for kickball. "But even though Nancy solves most of the capers, Ned *does* have a really nice car."

"Maybe we could go as them," Steven concedes wanly. The wind rustles his hair and turns down his collar for a moment where I notice a large red welt on his neck.

"Are you allergic to something?"

"No. Why?"

"Well, what happened to your neck?"

"Nothing."

"I just saw it—" but when I reach for his coat, Steven pushes me sharply away.

"Go play kickball. I know you want to."

"No, I don't. I want to play demon-possessed My Little Ponies."

"Well, we can't play that anymore. Aren't you listening?" Now his pink cheeks are flaming red, and even Steven seems surprised by the force of his voice, the way he spits a little as the words shoot forth from his mouth.

"Can you please just tell me what happened?" I ask, touching my own neck where the welt arose on his.

Steven hesitates, watches Mrs. Reid and Mrs. Blakenship circling the playground with their whistles in hand. "I got punished last night," he says finally.

"I know. It took forever to scrub the mud out of that carpet."

"No—by my father—after he came home. And it wasn't just for the carpet either."

"For what then?"

"If I don't start acting more like a boy, they might take away my piano lessons."

"But—"

Steven raises his hand like a stop sign, and I can see he is trembling, or shivering. Sometimes it is hard to tell the difference. "The next time we play house, I have to be the husband, OK?"

The Halloween problem is ultimately resolved when Steven and I decide to go to the party as pirates. I used to have to wear a patch on account of my bad eye, so I'm familiar with the process, and Steven's brother has a stuffed parrot we can borrow. Now I get to wear a peg-leg like I've always wanted, and Steven gets to wear bangles and a kerchief without any of the adults getting mad. In November, we help Steven's mother stuff a cornucopia with dried leaves and arrange ornamental gourds on her front porch to show how grateful we are. I have won back the trust I nearly lost with the mud and the My Little Ponies, and Steven says his father hasn't hit him for almost a month now.

"I'm learning a new aria, too," he boasts. "Do you want to hear it?"

"Sure. Do you want to kiss me first?" I ask.

"What for?"

"I think it would be fun," I say. "Nancy Drew kisses Ned Nickerson, and they seem to like it a lot."

Steven and I stand facing each other in his playroom, the rain splashing hard against the windows. He pushes up on his toes and presses his pursed lips against mine. The kiss is so quick and dry that neither of us is sure it has really happened.

"Do-over," I say. "I think you're supposed to turn your head more—and open your mouth."

"We'll get germs," Steven protests. He repeats the kiss the exact same way, and I am relieved to learn I'm not missing anything after all. "Now do you want to hear the song?"

I nod. This time I stand by the piano lid so I can watch the strings pull taut and go slack as Steven presses the keys.

"You don't think it's girly to play the piano, do you?"

"I think it's girly for boys to do ballet," I tell him honestly, "but not swimming or track, and definitely not piano. Everybody likes music."

Steven seems satisfied with this response and begins to play. In the aria, he gets to use the damper pedal and the soft pedal, which mutes the harshest, heaviest sounds. "The soft pedal is my favorite," he explains. "I bet Florence Nightingale would like it, too."

Then, it is Christmastime, and Steven and I are decorating the playroom tree with strings of popcorn and candy canes. We have draped some festive garland around the piano bench, and even Johnny and Amanda wear jaunty red-and-green bows. Steven has just begun to play "The Little Drummer Boy" when Mrs. Mann appears in the doorway, her cardigan buttoned to maximum constriction, her hair more unmoving than ever.

Steven's hands freeze on the keyboard, and I feel myself shrinking deep in my loafers like the bad witch in *The Wizard of Oz*.

"Julie, I'd like to see you upstairs a moment."

"Should I come, too?" Steven asks.

"No, dear. Stay right there and keep practicing."

I know I must have done something awful, but I can't think what it could be ... unless ... *the kiss!* Girls aren't supposed to make the first move, but I had talked Steven into it, and then I dared him to do it again under the mistletoe, and that time we made our tongues touch and held them together to the count of five.

Mrs. Mann leads me down the long corridor toward Steven's room, but at the last minute, we veer off into her bedroom, a privileged space I have never even connived to enter before. The air is thick and sweet with grown-woman perfume, and the carpet is so plush it feels like wearing slippers all the time. There are two, straight-backed chairs arranged around a tiny, circular table, and Mrs. Mann instructs me to sit down on one of them while she positions herself across from me on the other. I half-expect a butler to emerge from the closet and offer us a cup of tea.

"Now, do you have any idea why I've summoned you, and why I've done so out of earshot of both of my children?"

I shake my head, watching her lips move like the dark red lips in the Twizzlers commercials.

"It has to do with something I overheard you saying to Steven the other day in the basement."

But I say so many things! I wait for her to be more specific.

"Julie, do you recall telling Steven that boys and girls aren't the only kinds of people in the world?"

"Yes." I have to fight very hard not to fidget with the trinkets on her table.

"Do you want to repeat for me exactly what it was you said—the message you intended to impart?"

"Well, I was just trying to cheer Steven up because he always gets picked last when we play kickball in PE—or really any sport—and so I said about how there are boy-boys like Carl Lull and girl-girls like Erin Saunders, but there are also kids like us who are somewhere in the middle."

"What do you mean by that—*in the middle?*" Her neatly trimmed eyebrows turn downward and meet in the middle of her forehead to form an angry V, but I sense I shouldn't use this as an example of a middle.

"I mean that we're more than one thing. I'm more of a girl-boy. Girl first because I'm actually a girl, but I have a little boy in me, too. That's why I'm so good at kickball. And Steven is a boy-girl because he's a boy, of course, but you know, he's got some girl in him. That's why sometimes he wishes he could wear a dress."

"What did you say?" Her mascara is beginning to run, and Mrs. Mann hurries to her night table to get a tissue.

"It's not like he wants to do *ballet*," I reassure her. "It's not like he wants to wear a *tutu*."

"I think I've heard about enough," and she is trembling for sure, twisting the fat diamond on her finger and growing red around her ears. "I've already called your mother to come and get you, and we'll be pulling Steven out of school right after the holidays."

"But you can't!" I protest. "We're going to dress up as two pieces of one heart on Valentine's Day and two leaves each of a four-leaf clover on St. Patrick's Day!" Steven and I have the whole year's costumes planned in advance.

But Mrs. Mann won't hear another word. As she rises to her feet, I realize with growing horror that Mrs. Mann is also wearing loafers, exactly like mine but larger. "Mr. Mann and I have to do what is in Steven's best interest. We can't have someone like you jeopardizing his entire future and filling his head with—"

She stands before me, looking fragile as one of her porcelain trinkets, small and thin with her slacks cinched tight and her little gold cross glimmering between the strained cords of her neck. She no longer seems menacing at all, but I still don't understand why she is so afraid.

When my mother comes, she and Mrs. Mann go into the kitchen and close the sliding door. Steven and I creep up the stairs and lie flat on our bellies, listening.

"I don't know what kind of permissive parenting you practice at your house, but my husband is *furious* with the kind of lies your daughter is telling!"

Now my mother takes up for me, much to my delighted surprise: "Julie may have a colorful imagination, but she's been raised right!"

"Has she? Well, I'm glad to see you're proud of your little lesbian, but I'm not going to let my son turn out that way!"

"You've crossed a line, Susan. Don't you *dare* speak to me about my daughter like that when you have raised the *nanciest* little musician I've ever seen!"

Steven and I look at each other and then out across the deep, semantic void. "Maybe we should sit on your couch—cross-legged, with our shoes on—just to teach them a lesson." But I am only half-serious, and Steven understands the difference between a strong wish and an act with consequences.

"I'll miss you," he murmurs. "I'll write a song for you and play it on TV like Yanni." Steven looks a lot more like John Tesh, but I know better than to interfere with his dreams.

"I'll go as Florence Nightingale for Halloween next year," I promise, then pinky-swear, "and you can go as a bullfighter for me."

On the ride home, I sit in the back seat of my mother's Pinto station wagon just as I always do—on the middle hump between the two lower cushions, my seat belt cold and only loosely fastened. The trees we pass are mostly tall and green, always green, and pointed toward the sky like spears. Just because people string lights through the branches this time of year doesn't mean that subtle hint of violence disappears.

When I look toward the rearview mirror, I see how my mother's makeup has stained her face like a notebook left out in the rain. When she catches my gaze, she sniffs a little, then tries to force a smile.

"That Mrs. Mann is a real piece of work. Wait till your father hears about this."

"Am I in trouble, Mom?" I ask, preparing myself for the worst.

"Why would *you* be in trouble? It's not your fault that Steven Mann is—"

Then, she stops, meets my eyes in the mirror, and neither one of us wants her to finish that sentence. There are so many questions I could ask my mother, and so many answers she could demand of me. Instead, she turns the radio on, and we drive home through a new downpour, humming "Have Yourself a Merry Little Christmas" softly along with Judy Garland.

This is before I break my promise to Steven Mann and go as the bullfighter I really want to be for Halloween. This is before I become captain of the kickball team, before I bury the My Little Ponies somewhere in the backyard and then forget where. And this is long before I meet Steven Mann again at a Dairy Queen in fourth grade.

He is still blond and sweet-faced, though his freckles are fading, and he has this way of looking over his shoulder and hunching like he's dodging a ball. That's how our eyes meet, how I tug him out of line and over to the table where I'm sitting alone. It's one of those birthday parties where the girl has to invite everyone in her class. She doesn't want me there. He has a free token and offers to share his sundae.

This is before Steven Mann tells me everything in his life is going just fine, then flushes red as the DQ sign. We both know that he is lying.

"Are you still playing piano?" I ask.

He doesn't answer. Instead, he stands, tucks his hands deep in his pocket, then draws one out again—the right one—and extends it to me. "My mom'll be here any minute, so I should probably go and wait outside."

I put my hand in his, and he squeezes it hard. I can't tell if he is trying to hurt me or if he just wants to show me how strong he is.

This is before I never see Steven Mann again, before everyone pretends they don't remember him. This is before.

Mrs. Saunders

[Or a Study of Origins in Odd and Even Numbers]

About some women the comment was reverently made, "Mrs. So-and-So was born to be a mother." At first, this was hard for me to grasp, since we were born daughters, not mothers, and we would remain daughters our whole lives, no matter what else we did, even if one day without any warning, we turned into mothers ourselves.

Take my mother, for instance. Did she not lean on the counter with one eye closed and fluttering, the phone's hard yellow casing pressed against her ear, the calendar splayed open before her? Did she not fidget and squirm like a restless child, biting down on her pencil until it splintered, then reply in a gravelly impersonation of her own voice, "Yes, Mother, yes, *all right*, I'll be there." Shocking though it seemed, every mother was also somebody's daughter.

Not every daughter was somebody's mother, though. Take my Aunt Linda, for instance—daughter of my grandmother, sister to my father, and mother of precisely no one at all. She moved through the world unencumbered, zipping around town in her sleek, gold Mustang, never calling for a babysitter when she went out on a Saturday night. There were no Mr. Yuk stickers on the cleaning products under her sink—I had checked—and no sippy cups or Krazy Straws interspersed with the fine white China in her cabinets.

"Yes, but notice," my mother said, "your Aunt Linda has no pictures on her refrigerator." It was true, I marveled. The door was shiny, brown, and bare, so clean I could see my own reflection. Was it possible Aunt Linda didn't even own a set of colorful, alphabet magnets? Taking out the Crayolas from my travel kit, I resolved to sketch something for her right away.

To make matters more complicated still, of the daughters who grew up to be mothers, not every one of these was deemed "a natural." According to the umpires of the parenting game, some mothers worried too much, and, as a result, their babies never stopped spitting up or stayed bald until their preschool years. Some mothers were always distracted, so their babies developed the croup as a shameless plea for attention. Some mothers, my father decreed, "were really still children themselves." Their babies couldn't fall asleep without a pacifier and arrived at kindergarten still dragging their blankies behind them. A few mothers were even rumored to lack that renowned "maternal instinct," which I had known to transform ordinary dough into magnificent chocolate chip cookies.

Among the born-to-be mothers, I had singled out Mrs. Saunders for MVP. Hers was a pretty, round face with a mouth that seemed always to be smiling, a body plush and huggable at the center as a favorite stuffed animal, and her fingernails painted a pleasing shade of pink—nice to look at and skillful, too, for unraveling thread or unclasping necklaces. Mrs. Saunders drove a bright blue station wagon that could always accommodate more children, and if you were lucky, you got to sit on the tiny seat beside the wheel well, blissfully unbuckled, watching the tree-lined road recede behind you like the trailer of an old-fashioned, grown-up film.

Mrs. Saunders always came early and stayed late and offered to chaperone on field trips to the Ballard Locks or the Seattle Aquarium. If you cried, she had a tissue. If you spilled something, she had a moist toilette. If your tummy hurt, she would rock you on her lap and let your head fall against the soft balloons of her chest. She knew the words to all the best songs ("The Itsy, Bitsy Spider,"

"Row, Row, Row Your Boat") and the rules to all the best games (Chutes and Ladders, Hi-Ho! Cherry-O), and there wasn't anything she couldn't cook by the dozen or scrub to spotless and gleaming in seconds. Her purse was the size of a train's caboose and contained, among so many wonderful things, a preponderance of red, individually wrapped boxes of Sun-Maid raisins and sometimes, if you were especially good, a gum-filled lollipop.

If Mrs. Saunders was born to be a mother, then Erin Saunders was surely born to be a daughter—or better said, it came naturally to her, this business of being a girl. She hated bugs and mud, was grossed out easily, and wouldn't splash in puddles without her polka dot galoshes. She always insisted on washing her hands immediately after finger painting and liked hats with large brims for days when there was lots of sun. Erin asked for pierced ears on her sixth birthday and got them—a little set of golden hoops as dainty as her own set of little, golden ears—and she seemed to know instinctively that Cabbage Patch dolls should be requested for Christmas. The more closely the doll resembled the girl she belonged to, the better it was for both of them. This resemblance should be striking and obvious, right down to their clothing, accessories, and hair style. Erin's doll had thin blond hair swept up in a side ponytail, wide cerulean eyes, and dimples that framed her chin. She wore patterned leggings and long, single-tone sweatshirts with jelly bracelets on her fabric wrists. Her name was Erina, her nickname "the Ballerina," and in the early years, I never once saw Erin without her.

Koosh balls and Teddy Ruxbins were a different story. "They're for boys," Erin said, empowered by the quiet authority of her position as Ultimate Girl.

"But how do you know?" I asked her.

Erin shrugged, then smoothed a lump of Play-Doh with a miniature rolling pin as she began to mold it into a loaf of pink bread.

"What about Play-Doh?" I challenged. "Both boys and girls can play with that."

"Yes, but—it depends what they make with it." I watched her slicing the bread with a plastic knife, then spreading it out on the top of her desk. "See, it's a picnic, just like the ones I take with my mom."

* * *

I always felt uneasy when people said, "Like mother, like daughter," as if this were some kind of given, some irrefutable truth. Of course I could see why Erin would imagine herself like her mother—why she would *want* to be—but the story didn't seem quite so simple to me. Mrs. Saunders was fragrant and warm, a soft body in baggy jeans and sweatshirts with white, frilled collars sewn in. She smiled without reservation and worked tirelessly to put everyone around her at ease. The same could not be said of Erin, or of her sister Julia, an elusive fifth-grader with fine black hair who kept her eyes down and her pale face tilted away. Both girls passed under the protective veil of shy, claiming a delicacy I found dubious and vexing somehow—their bodies pinched tight and impossibly narrow, their limbs long and their faces small. Even in first grade, boys tripped over their laces trying to make Erin laugh, and girls mused how they could always lift her, "the lightest girl in the class."

On this particular day, only my mother's back was visible, her floral apron knotted twice at the waist, as I wandered into the kitchen and took my place at the table.

"Apple slices or fruit cocktail?" she asked without turning around.

"Fruit cocktail, please," I replied. As I opened my notebook, I anticipated the pleasant sound of a Tupperware top coming unsealed, the slosh of the grapes and peaches in sweetened syrup as they slid from the tub to the bowl, and all this followed by the satisfying clank of a spoon. But instead my mother lifted a heavy can down from the shelf, grunting as she cranked our can opener by its slow and rusty arm.

"I think you like me to struggle," she muttered, but when I switched to apple slices instead, she informed me the hard part was already done.

"Mom, why do storks always stand on one leg?" We had been reading a Hans Christian Andersen story at school, and in all the pictures, the storks stood proudly on rooftops and weathervanes with one foot raised and tucked beneath their feathers.

"How should I know?" she said, placing the bowl beside me but forgetting to bring a spoon. My mother hovered over me then, and I considered her reflection in the glass tabletop—the sweat pooling on her upper lip, the sharp crease between her brows. "Is this an assignment for school?"

"No, it's a new picture for Aunt Linda," I beamed. "See—there's her apartment building," a black column with many windows, "and these are the telephone poles with all their wires, and here's a stork flying from far away." In the background, I had colored a huge yellow moon to spotlight the stork and the city landscape.

"What is that stork doing there?" my mother asked, leaning in so close I could smell the home permanent juice in her hair.

"Storks bring the babies," I explained. "Maybe someday a stork will bring Aunt Linda a baby of her very own."

Just then my father's face appeared in the glass, and I watched as he kissed my mother's ear and cracked an imaginary egg on my head. "How was your day, Smidge?" he asked.

"Bill, do you see what she's drawing here?" My mother's cheeks scorched—brighter than her rouge, and darker, too. This color always portended a change in mood.

"Looks terrific," he said, stealing the half slice of garish red cherry from my bowl.

"Daddy, could I please have a spoon?"

He nodded and padded away to the silverware drawer.

"No, it is *not* terrific," my mother replied, her hands settling like angry white birds on her hips. "Storks do *not* deliver babies to unmarried women."

"But Dumbo's mother wasn't married," I said, and continued shading the night sky with lacy swirls of gray. "I don't even think Dumbo had a father."

Exasperated, my mother turned to my father, who scratched his sideburns and peered down at my page. "Your mother's right, Julie," he confirmed at last. "You do have to be married to have a baby."

"But what about Dumbo?"

"They're *elephants!* They don't get married. Draw something else for your aunt."

"But Aunt Linda could still get married, couldn't she? She might meet someone and fall in love."

"Unlikely," my mother scoffed, and my father flashed her his best cease-and-desist look.

"Maybe I could just save the picture for her until she does."

"This is not an open negotiation. Do as you're told," my mother replied, tossing an invisible pizza into the air.

I sighed, repeating the motion as she turned away. Was it mimicry? Was it instinct? This was hard to say. My father laughed from his belly, nervous and loud. "Like mother, like daughter," he said.

Though I couldn't see my mother's face, I felt our thick lips, in unison, twisting into a scowl.

* * *

A few weeks later, Erin Saunders invited me to play at her house after school. "But it isn't even your birthday yet," I answered, perplexed, the only reasonable explanation for this gesture of inclusion.

"My mother said I should ask you now so you can get permission from your mother," she shrugged. "You don't have to come if you don't want to."

I watched the tiny diamonds glittering in her ears. I couldn't tell if they were supposed to be rabbits or butterflies. "OK, I'll ask her."

"Oh, and if you have any roller skates," Erin said, looking past me to the playground, her eyes always searching for a better place to be, "you should bring them with you."

"Roller skates?"

"My sister and I like to roller-skate a lot after school."

At home, I set to rummaging. My father was mowing the lawn, and my mother had gone with her mother, Grandma Tena, to a garden club meeting. She would return at dinnertime in a mood for slamming doors and severing the straps from handbags. If I stole a glance at her face, even a quick over-the-shoulder glance in the bedroom mirror, I would notice how gummy her lashes were—one of the tell-tale signs of weeping while wearing mascara. Then, I would want to say something comforting, but I would bring a cup of tea instead—water heated in the microwave, a pack of Lemon Zinger on the saucer. My hands would shake as I set it on the table. Where my mother was concerned, I could never trust my words to come out right.

In the meantime, I stuffed my duffel bag with two Get in Shape Girl wristbands, one Get in Shape Girl headband, a leotard, tights, fuzzy pink legwarmers, and the only pair of roller skates I owned. They were for beginners—old skates from Fisher Price, flat on top with orange wheels and blue buckles that clasped around your shoes—not like the lace-up kind we borrowed at the rink. Was there anything else I could need for a visit at Erin Saunders' house? I scanned my room for something to impress her and settled on the most girlish of all my possessions: a floral jewelry box with a full-skirted ballerina inside. I liked to lay my head on the dresser and watch my own hand guiding the lid slowly closed, the music winding down to its final, hesitant whine.

The ballerina, come to think of it, looked a little like Erin Saunders—thin as a blade of grass with lips set in a bow. The best part was watching her body fold in on itself, the crumpling of a note or a wilted corsage until suddenly, she was flat, she was smashed, she was dead, and only when I chose to raise the lid could she be resurrected—like a little tulle soldier—springing to upright attention again.

* * *

The next day at three o'clock dismissal, I looked out the window to find Mrs. Saunders already parked and leaning against her car, chatting amiably with some of the other mothers. I walked toward her the way a deer approaches a rare person in the forest—curiously, but with restraint. Then, slowly, her hand unfurled, and she was holding out to me a sacred offering—a little red box of Sun-Maid raisins.

"Hop in!" she smiled, and so I did, wedging my bag behind the driver's seat and resting my feet lightly on top.

Soon, Julia slid in beside me through the other door, accompanied by a gaunt sixth grader named Ashley. Neither of them looked at me but continued their conversation through low murmurs and pantomimes. Their laughter came at intervals, high-pitched like Snow White's voice in the cartoon movie. But where was Erin? I pressed my face to the glass, and that's when I saw her, emerging from the building at last, a half-zipped Jansport dangling from her arm and Lana Steeley clasping her one free hand.

"Come on, girls!" Mrs. Saunders waved, and like Siamese twins, they glided across the asphalt in one synchronized movement before tugging open the rear door to the station wagon.

"You're riding in back, then?" Mrs. Saunders confirmed, handing them each a pack of raisins. She closed the door with enough force that the whole car wobbled a little before she assumed her place behind the steering wheel, which was covered with golden fur like a lion's mane.

On the ride to Erin Saunders' house, I began to compute the uneasy math of my situation: 2+2+1. We were learning about even numbers and odd numbers in Miss Campbell's class, and the way I understood it was, if you had to pair off for a game and everyone in the group had a partner, the number was even. If you had to pair off and there was one person left standing alone, drawing dust circles on the pavement with her shoe, the number was odd, and the person with the dirty shoe was odd, too. That's why they called her the "odd girl out."

The Saunders lived in a plain yellow house in Arbor Heights with a gravel driveway and shaky wooden stairs leading to a front door framed on both sides by glass. When we arrived, just as I feared, both pairs of girls bolted evenly up the stairs, their ponytails swishing, and disappeared to places where they hoped they wouldn't be found. I helped Mrs. Saunders lug in the groceries and then stood marveling at her majestic silver refrigerator with its wardrobe-style double doors and square portal for dispensing water and ice.

"I'm sure Erin and Lana are down in the basement. Did you bring your roller skates?" she asked.

I nodded, still transfixed by the stark elegance of the appliance. Then, as if startled awake: "But Mrs. Saunders, you're a *mother!*"

"Why, yes, I am," she laughed, handing me a chilled Capri Sun.

"Where are the pictures for your refrigerator?"

"Oh, they're over there, dear—on the bulletin board," she said, pointing to a large cork panel that stretched along the breakfast nook wall. "This new kind of fridge doesn't have good stick for magnets." I noted a rainbow assortment of push pins held the pretty drawings in place.

"Here," Mrs. Saunders instructed. "You take a juice pouch for Erin and Lana. Go ahead—don't be shy. Right down those stairs over there." My duffel drooped on my shoulder, a wilted lavender flower, and I couldn't help looking back even as my feet shuffled slowly forward. The basement posed a problem I knew I couldn't solve: 2+1 still equaled odd girl out.

I heard the whooshing sound of their skates on the smooth concrete before I caught the blur of their faces. Perching on the bottom step, I waited, but Erin and Lana just kept skating in graceful loops, their cheeks turning mauve, then maroon. Finally, I cleared my throat.

"Your mom sent down some Capri Suns. Would you like one?"

The girls skated toward me, fearless and fast, and at the last possible moment, tipped their skates down on the brakes that were shaped like bells. I flinched, and Lana snickered. "Did you think we were going to hit you?"

"Maybe," I said, as they lifted the drinks out of my hand.

"Put on your skates," Erin directed. Then, she shimmied backwards while sliding the straw effortlessly into the pre-made hole.

Such coordination had always eluded me, so I turned the pouch upside down and speared its wide, silver middle.

Lana dawdled nearby, sipping her drink and staring hard at me as I began to unlace my shoes. "Are your curls real?" she asked.

"What do you mean?"

"Come on!" Erin pressed, spinning easy figure eights around the room. "Put on your skates."

"Your curls—are they real? And don't lie," Lana said, with a cocky twist of her hip. "I can always tell when people are lying."

My tongue turned to cotton in my mouth. On the one hand, my mother had taught me never to lie; on the other, she made me promise I would never reveal the secret behind our Toni Silkwave hair.

"Leave it alone, Lana," Erin whined. "You know we're supposed to be nice to her."

"Why?" I wasn't even stalling. "Why are you supposed to be nice to me?"

Erin scissored her legs back and forth in slow motion. I stood and began to walk toward her in my stocking feet, leaving little sweaty footprints on the floor.

She sighed and flattened the juice pouch with a last, pouty swallow. "My mom says we have to be nice to you because your mom got hate mail and had a hysterectomy."

"A what?" My breath came in little gasps. The light streaming in through all the windows began to seem too bright. When I looked back at Lana, she was going through my things.

"These are the weirdest roller skates ever," she said, holding them up so Erin could see. "And why did you bring ballet clothes and a jewelry box?"

I turned to Erin, but she wasn't in the same spot anymore. She was gliding around the room again, and I had to spin on my heels to follow.

"What did you say about my mom? It's important. I need to know."

"Some of the other mothers don't like her, I guess, and one of them sent her a note. But my mom says I'm not supposed to tell you."

"I don't care about that," I said, trying to be brave for my mother's sake. Maybe there was an odd number of mothers, and she was left with her toe in the dirt, a grown-up odd girl out. "You said another word—what was it?"

Erin spun around one of the dark gray poles. "Oh, that just means she can't have any more babies." *Every night I prayed for a brother or a sister. I rocked on my knees till they were rug-burned, begging God not to leave me alone.* "My mom says the baby needs a nest to grow, and your mom doesn't have her nest anymore." *One was the oddest number.*

Just then, the room began to swivel, but I was standing still. I heard thunder in my ears, but the afternoon was quiet. The next thing I knew, I was lying on the floor, and Lana Steeley was leaning over me, one of my tight ringlets coiled around her thumb. "I think you fainted," she said. "And your head smells like a beauty salon."

Mrs. Saunders gave me chewable, orange-flavored Tylenol for the pain in my head and called my mother to pick me up as soon as she could. I left the house with a gum-filled lollipop and an ice pack pressed to the back of my skull.

"Why do you think you fainted?" my mother asked. "That isn't like you." She didn't sound angry or sympathetic either. More than anything, she seemed surprised.

"I fainted once," she told me, as we coasted over the long hills home. "It was before you were born, and I was sitting on a stool in my classroom, just reading a story, and all of a sudden, I collapsed on the floor. One of my students ran to get the principal, and he told her Mrs. Wade was dead."

It was all too much to take in: the idea of my mother before I was born, the idea of my mother as *Mrs. Wade,* the idea of my mother dead. I pictured her like the flat ballerina in the jewel box. They even wore the same shade of Wet 'n' Wild lipstick and Cover Girl rouge.

"You and Dad are still married, right?" I ventured.

Her eyes fixed on mine in the rearview. "Whatever gave you the idea that we weren't? Just because your father has to travel for work doesn't have anything to do with our marriage."

"I don't know," I said, taking a slow breath. For some reason—I didn't know why—my mother was touchy about this subject. "I guess I just wish he was around more."

"Well, you'll have him all day Saturday because Grandma and I are going to the Plant Expo."

"Why do you like plants so much?" I asked, biting through the hard candy shell of my lollipop to the soft pink bubblegum center.

"They're lovely to look at," my mother replied. "And they don't want more from me than I can give."

* * *

My mother had always referred to me as a "Daddy's girl," and I could hear the flame flickering in her throat as she said it. Sometimes, when she was angry with me for something else, like leaving a ring of scum around the bathtub or dropping silverware on the new linoleum floor, she would say, her lashes turning gummy again, "You just don't care, do you? From the moment you were born, you were already looking past me to your father."

On Saturday morning, I stood in line at Winchell's Donut House, my father tall as a steeple behind me, his hands resting lightly on my shoulders. "Do you know what you want, Smidge?" he asked.

Yes, I knew. Of course I knew. I wanted a round white donut with rainbow sprinkles and a brand-new baby brother or sister. "Just tell the lady what you want," he said, and I studied his reflection in the display case—his white teeth and wide smile, the small pouches under his eyes that my mother said were a sign of being overtired.

"Are you OK, Daddy?" I asked him as we settled into our favorite corner booth.

"Never been better." He grinned at me, unzipping his parka. "What about *you*? How's my favorite first grader?"

"Satisfactory, but not superior," I replied, thinking of the categories for evaluation on my new report card. "Miss Campbell is not as nice as Mrs. Shields, and Selena Barth told everyone I'm a know-it-all, and I fainted at Erin Saunders' house on Tuesday after school."

"Your mom mentioned that. She said she thought you were probably hungry, and—"

"No, I wasn't!" The force of my own voice startled me. Not only that, but my chest and throat were beginning to swelter beneath the thick wool of my turtleneck sweater. "I *wasn't* hungry. I was upset because Erin Saunders told me that Mom is never going to have another baby. *Ever.* The stork won't come to our house because she doesn't have a nest, even though the two of you are married and everything."

A tear leapt out of my eye and landed on the little square of wax paper that held my rainbow-sprinkle donut.

"Hey, hey," my father said, stretching his hands across the table. "Slow down. Let's not panic. What's all this about a baby?"

"Everyone else has a brother or a sister. The stork comes to everyone else's house. And we have a chimney *and* a weathervane!" The people around us looked up, mid-bite, from their maple bars and apple fritters. "I prayed for God to send the stork, and I know babies take a long time to get made, but—"

This was something I loved about my father: whenever I started to cry, he always let me finish, even if we were in a public place and I was, as my mother would say, "making a scene." When the tears slowed to just a trickle, he would reach into his pocket and produce a white handkerchief embroidered with his initials, *WSW*. I could use this instead of my sleeve for wiping my nose and eyes.

"I'm sorry," he said finally. He sipped his coffee, sighed, looked out at the rest of Westwood Village, then brought his eyes back to rest on mine. "I thought your mother and I had explained this to you before. I know we've both tried . . ." My father reached into his pocket again, but this time he pulled out his wallet and laid it open on the table. "Do you remember when this picture was taken?"

I recognized myself in a striped shirt and pigtails perched on the kitchen counter. I held the phone in the crook of my shoulder, but the receiver was upside down. "No," I said, blotting my face again and shaking my head.

"I took this picture when you were talking on the phone with your mother. You don't remember, huh? Well, it was a long time ago, and she's all better now, but your mom was in the hospital to have a major surgery, and that surgery means she won't be able to have another baby. We always planned on two children," he said, "but we feel very lucky that we got to have you."

My voice was quiet now, and desperate. I still hadn't touched my donut. "What about the stork? Couldn't he just bring the baby anyway?"

"Here's the thing, Julie," my father said. "Remember when we talked about the bald eagle that you saw on that flag at the fair?" I nodded. "And I told you that the eagle represents freedom, represents our whole country, the whole United States. It's a symbol of what we believe in as a people, right?" I nodded again. "Well, you need to think of the stork that way, too. The stork is a *symbol*—of family, of new babies coming into a family—but the stork doesn't actually bring the babies."

"So, it's a lie?" I said, incredulous, feeling the itchy heat under my shirt again.

"It's not a lie. It's a story—like Little Red Riding Hood or Snow White or Sleeping Beauty. Those aren't lies; they're stories." He pushed my donut toward me. "Part of growing up is learning to tell the difference."

* * *

Everyone knew the best kind of mother to be was a "natural," but the most exciting kind of mother to be was "expecting." I used to think it meant that the woman was expecting a visit from the stork, but now I had to reconsider.

When we jumped rope at recess, everyone chanted the name of the girl who was jumping and the name of a boy from our class, a boy they thought she liked or a boy who might like her. Erin, unsurprisingly, was a gifted jumper and always preferred double Dutch: "Erin and Justin sitting in a tree, K-I-S-S-I-N-G! First comes love, then comes marriage, then comes baby in the baby carriage!"

This, too, was a math problem, like the addition pop quizzes we took when Miss Campbell set the big white timer at the front of the room and told us to calculate as fast as we could: LOVE + MARRIAGE = BABY. The stork was just a symbol and didn't appear in the problem at all. So, if my parents were married, why couldn't they have a baby? What were they missing if not the stork? I gulped as I made the deduction: *LOVE?*

Now Lana was jumping with Erin, side to side in their matching overalls and blinding white Keds. "Lana and Lee sitting in a tree, K-I-S-S-I-N-G! First comes love, then comes marriage, then comes baby in the baby carriage!" I realized then, looking at them, that they resembled the kids in commercials, the ones whose mothers used fancy, name-brand laundry detergents like Tide or Cheer to lift out spaghetti and meatball stains.

My mother bought in bulk and scooped our detergent from a fat pail without a label. We didn't have Bounce dryer sheets in their appealing orange box, just a clothesline outside for summer and a clothesline inside for the rest of the year.

It was my turn to jump, but I was still thinking about the simple arithmetic of LOVE + MARRIAGE and what my mother's surgery had to do with anything, least of all my plight as an only child. Had my father fed me a story or a lie with my Winchell's donut? I couldn't be sure. No one seemed trustworthy now. "Go!" Selena said, shoving me in between Erin and Lana where I promptly tripped and brought the whole game to a quick, embarrassing halt. One of the ropes swung around sharply and struck me in the face.

"Why don't you go play foursquare or something?" Selena sneered. "You're better at boys' games anyway."

"No, I want to jump," I insisted. "Give me another try." Erin and Lana reluctantly took up the rope—one rope only, for which I was relieved—and began to twirl it with exaggerated lethargy. Their twirl was so slow I could skip back and forth between my feet as they recited, "Julie and Steven sitting in a tree, K-I-S-S-I-N-G! First comes love, then comes marriage, then comes baby in the baby carriage!"

This time I heard the words a new way. I realized what they were actually saying. The chant was about each of us having our own babies someday—not brothers and sisters, but children that would belong to us when we were children no longer. I looked across the playground at Steven Mann, turning his toes in dust as the other boys kicked a ball and ran around the bases. He was like me. He understood. In the shade, I noticed a group of girls pushing little pink strollers in a circle, rocking the dolls in their arms with plastic baby bottles and then lifting them up to their shoulders to burp them. Suddenly, it was as if the big white timer had gone off in my head, abrupt and disconcerting. When I took Amy, my bald, sailor-suited baby doll, with me to the store, I never pretended she was *my* baby. I played the dutiful big sister, tending her in the cart while my mother thumped cantaloupes or demanded the cashier call a manager. When I was grown, I wouldn't need her anymore. I'd have a car and a checkbook and a St. Bernard. I could draw my own pictures for the refrigerator door.

Then, it was full spring. All the girlish trees dripped their fragrant pink blossoms, and Erin Saunders announced to the whole class she was having a slumber party. "All the girls are invited," she said, "on account of how that's the rule. We're going swimming at the Arbor Heights pool, so bring your swimsuit and towel, and you should also bring your sleeping bag and pillow."

"Do you have anything else to share with the class?" Miss Campbell nudged, opening her third Diet Coke of the morning and flashing Erin a rare smile.

Erin shrugged and twirled her hair, looking past Miss Campbell to her cubby.

"You're sure you don't have any news to share . . . maybe something about a new addition to your family?"

"Oh," Erin sighed. "*That.* My mom's expecting another baby." She rolled her eyes and whispered to Lana, "I am *not* going to share my room."

"I think that deserves a round of applause, don't you?" Miss Campbell addressed the class, tapping her one free hand against the sweating can of soda. The other kids began to clap, but I silently refused. The heat in my belly rose up behind my eyes, burning them from the inside out. Then, with one furious motion, I stabbed my pencil through the Pink Pearl eraser on the corner of my desk. It stayed there like that, unwavering, even when I took my hands away.

There were seven guests at Erin Saunders' sleepover, which meant three pairs of girls and one extra. They were Erin and Lana, Selena and Megan, Amanda and Shannon, plus me. We hadn't gotten to remainders in division yet, and wouldn't for several years, but already I knew how the number after the decimal felt.

Mr. Saunders drove us back from the pool in his plumber's van, where we sat in staggered L-shapes along the windowless walls. He played the radio the whole time and never said a word to any of us. I watched how he kept time with the music on the steering wheel, his big thumbs drumming along, but he didn't sing. Language he reserved entirely for the curses he spat at other drivers.

Back at the house, Mrs. Saunders was baking cookies and drinking orange juice, something pregnant women always did in Tropicana commercials. She wore denim overalls like the kind popular among girls our age, except hers were much bigger and her belly protruded so far it seemed to strain the pockets. "I'll be in the shower," Mr. Saunders said, dropping his heavy lunch box on the counter.

"OK, honey," she told him. "I have your dinner warming in the oven." He grunted something I couldn't hear as he lumbered up the stairs. Turning to us, Mrs. Saunders smiled, sighed, and wiped the sweat from her face with the nearest dish towel. "Why don't you girls go down to the basement and lay out your sleeping bags? The TV and VCR are all set up, and I'll send Julia down in a little while with some cookies. I already took down the Hawaiian punch."

"Mom, Lana and I want to sleep in my bedroom," Erin said, fishing a chocolate chip out of the bowl of cookie dough.

"You girls can do that another time," Mrs. Saunders replied, "when Lana is your only guest. Now be a good hostess and show your friends where you're all going to sleep tonight."

Erin pulled her wet hair back in a banana clip and motioned for us to follow.

"Who wants to play Truth or Dare?" Lana asked when we were all shivering in our pajamas and stretched out on our sleeping bags like students in a late-night gym class.

Everyone looked at Erin, and when she raised her hand, the others did, too. I gave my elbow a little boost, since my instincts told me this was a dangerous game, and my hand wasn't going to lift on its own.

"If you pick Truth," Lana said, "you have to answer the question by saying 'I swear on my mother's grave,' OK? That's the only way to prove you aren't lying."

Even though Erin was the birthday girl, Lana had appointed herself captain of the party ship, commander-in-chief of the night's festivities. No one seemed to question her power.

"So, who wants to go first?" She chewed a licorice stick thoughtfully as she positioned herself in the center of the room. Kneeling on a couch cushion, she focused her eyes like two green laser beams on mine. "Julie, I think you should go first."

"Why?" I sputtered.

"This is your first slumber party, isn't it?" *How did she know?* I wondered. "Is that my question for the Truth or Dare?"

"Are you kidding?" Lana laughed. "We're going to ask you something *much* harder than that. But first," she said, sitting back on her heels, "you get to ask a question of anybody in the room. Before you ask it, make sure to say 'Truth or Dare.'"

I wanted to know the truth about babies and where exactly they came from if it wasn't the stork and how once the baby got inside the woman it was able to get out and why it was able to breathe for so long in a place like that when Cherie on *Punky Brewster* had just recently almost died when she got trapped inside an old refrigerator. I also wanted to know what any of this had to do with love and marriage and men and women. But these were so many questions— hard questions—and I was known to be the best in my class at all the timed math drills, so if I didn't have the answers, what were the odds that these girls did?

"I have a question for Erin," I said finally. "Truth or Dare?"

"Truth," she said, her arms wrapped around her pillow in a posture of cool indifference.

"What do you know about the hate mail that was sent to my mom? You have to swear on your mother's grave that you'll tell me everything you know."

"This again," Erin sighed, causing her wispy bangs to flutter. "I swear, on my mother's grave"—I tried to picture Mrs. Saunders like the ballerina in the box, but I couldn't—she didn't belong there— "to tell you what I know."

"*Everything*," I clarified.

"*Everything*," she repeated. "My mom said that someone else's mother, probably Jennifer Rogge's but she's not sure, wrote your mom a letter and left it in her mailbox at school. When your mom got it, she started to cry, and my mother asked what was wrong, and your mother showed it to her. Basically, the letter said that your mom wears too much makeup to be a good Christian and is setting a bad example for all the girls at school by being so bossy and over-decorated. The letter called her the West Seattle Christian Clown."

The other girls gaped at each other. Clearly, it was the first they had heard about the letter, all except for Lana Steeley who only pretended to stifle a giggle but was obviously enjoying the scene.

"Now *we* get to ask you a question," she announced, "and I think we all know what that question is going to be."

"We do?" Amanda looked up from braiding Shannon's hair.

"*Yes*," Lana confirmed, her lips stained audaciously red with punch. "Truth or Dare?" I didn't want to call boys on the phone or toilet-paper a house or run around the block in my underwear, so I chose Truth. "You're sure? Really?" Lana asked.

I nodded, slowly, tearing off my nails one by one.

"We want to know if those are your real curls. Remember—you have to swear on your mother's grave."

I studied their faces like matching buttons on a sweater. They weren't identical, but they were interchangeable somehow. Like, if every face in the room was a button, and you lost one, any of the other button-faces would do.

Just then, we saw Julia's feet in her minty green scrunch socks descending the stairs. "Mom made you these cookies, Erin," she said, "and here's that movie I rented, *Three Men and a Baby*. It's supposed to have the ghost of a dead little kid in it or something. Ashley and I watched it. Pretty boring overall, but Tom Selleck is a mega-hunk."

"What's *Three Men and a Baby*?" I asked, my attention immediately piqued.

"Not so fast," Lana grinned, tapping her button nose. "You have to swear on your mother's grave. *Then,* we can watch the movie."

It didn't seem fair. The only way to protect my mother's secret was to risk her life. The only way to save her life was to break my promise that I would never tell. She could be struck by lightning right then, if I didn't confess. She might be sitting in bed with hot rollers in her hair, reading *Redbook* magazine, and all at once, she would spontaneously combust. Her heart could short-circuit. And then Mrs. Wade would be really and truly dead.

But did it happen as fast as all that? Would it actually happen at all? Was the "swear on your mother's grave"—meaning tell the truth or your mother dies—a true story in itself, or was it just another lie? I sucked in as much air as I could swallow and then I spat out as fast as I could, "I swear on my mother's grave that this is my real, natural-curly hair that I've had since the day I was born!" I watched Lana's dainty jaw unhinge, and she and Erin turned to each other, speechless at last.

* * *

The worst part of my first slumber party was definitely swearing a lie on my mother's grave, which was likely to result in her imminent or eventual death by terrifying circumstances beyond anyone's control. To tell the truth, I couldn't be sure whether I had lied to save her, or to save me, or simply to punish Lana for being so smug. But the best part of my first slumber party was definitely watching the movie *Three Men and a Baby.* In it, a pink, ruffled bassinette is left on the doorstep of three bachelors. None of the men is married or ever gets married, and no one seems to be in love with anyone else. Even at the end when the baby's mother returns, she doesn't marry the baby's father. Instead, the one woman and the three men all take the baby out for a walk in a supersize stroller they push together. It felt a little like Dorothy with the Scarecrow, the Tin Man, and the Lion, except, instead of Toto, they had this rosy, cheerful baby girl.

I didn't understand a lot of what happened in the rest of the story, but I decided that maybe it didn't matter so much where babies came from as where they might be acquired.

So, my mother didn't have a nest. So, the stork was really just a symbol. So, maybe love and marriage didn't have as much to do with babies as people wanted to believe. So what? The important thing now was to stop praying for God to make my mother pregnant and to start praying for another woman to change her mind about the baby she already had. Ours was such an inviting doorstep, I thought—the two stone flowerpots overflowing with pansies and petunias, the long walkway shaded by a little roof that kept us dry from rain.

Of all the places to leave a baby, I couldn't imagine a better one.

My mother was the last to arrive for morning pickup. Being punctual had never been her strong suit, but I found myself pacing just the same, peering out the living room window, watching the sky for phantom storms.

"I'm going to send you home with some cookies," Mrs. Saunders said, piling them on a plate and covering it with foil.

"Thank you," I said.

"How's your mother doing?" she asked, motioning for me to sit down at the table and draw.

"She's fine," I replied. "She's great even. She was just elected Vice-President of the West Seattle Garden Club. My grandmother was elected President."

"Well, good for her," Mrs. Saunders smiled, pouring herself another glass of orange juice. "I'm glad to hear it. She used to do a lot of substitute teaching at the school, but I don't see her as much anymore."

"She's just busy. She loves plants. She's very good at taking care of them."

Despite her mother's entreaties, Erin did not come downstairs to say good-bye. She and Lana were playing in her bedroom with the door closed and the music blaring, and my mother said we had several errands to run and couldn't stay.

"Did you have fun?" she asked me as I climbed into the back seat. I tried to shrug, to be casual the way that Erin was, but my mother didn't accept indifferent gestures. "Yes or no?" she demanded.

"It was fine," I said.

"But not great?"

"Not great, not terrible."

"The French have a saying for that," my mother offered. She majored in French in college and liked to teach me the words: "'Comme ci comme ça.' It means 'so-so,' but I think it sounds better in French, don't you?"

I nodded and then said "Yes" to make sure she heard me.

"I noticed you have a drawing there. Is that for Aunt Linda?"

I unrolled the yellow scroll of paper and appraised it proudly. I had drawn our front porch with the two flowerpots and the long walkway leading up to it, and there in the center before the dark red door, I had drawn a bassinette with a baby inside. It was perhaps my best drawing ever, and one of my last, since I had already discovered that putting words on paper was more satisfying than making pictures with markers or crayons.

"Actually," I said, letting the paper slip over the front seat, "I drew this one for you, Mom."

Mrs. Lennox

[Or a Study of Change as Crisis or Caricature]

Mrs. Lennox was married to Mr. Lennox, whose other name was Ted and who was the first adult I ever recognized as shy. When he brought Janna to swimming lessons, he sought a place away from the other parents—where he wouldn't be caught or required to talk, where he could look on and listen all alone.

It was the custom then to look for your watchers and wave at them, especially after you completed a dive. First came the succession of splashes; then our heads bobbed above the water in a row, and we scanned the steamy landscape till we found them—the ones we came with, the ones we belonged to. I saw my mother or my father, sometimes my father's mother, Grandma June, but I also cast a hopeful eye for Ted: the small, balding man standing in the bleachers' shadow, the thin fringe of hair curling up around his corduroy cap, the safety of his shirt-front—never audacious—navy blue and light gray plaid.

I always thought shyness was something you outgrew, like thumb-sucking or training wheels or letting people see you cry in public. But it was hard for Mr. Lennox to look people in the eye. It was hard for him to shake hands and smile and make chit-chat with the Dockered dads in their awkward semicircles on the lawn.

"Seems like a nice enough guy," I had heard my father say, "but damned if he isn't hard to get to know."

Mr. and Mrs. Lennox had two daughters. Heidi was older and blond and beguiling.

Janna was younger and blond and lacking her sister's sure footing, her effortless grace. The mothers noted how Mrs. Lennox "favored Heidi" and what a shame it was. "You always have a favorite," the mothers agreed. "But it's in bad taste to let your children know."

So, what did this mean for me, the one and only? What disappointments gleamed behind my mother's hard, blue eyes?

Mrs. Lennox was one of the mothers I didn't like. Perhaps a related fact: she was one of the mothers I sensed didn't like me. Whenever I played over at Janna's house and we sat up to the table for peanut butter and honey sandwiches on thick, grainy bread, Mrs. Lennox stood in the kitchen talking on the phone, the long cord curled around her fingers as she watched us, her expression sullen, her lips never turned up into a smile.

"What's your mom's real name?" I ask Janna, sitting on her bedroom rug and trimming the hair of her She-Ra dolls with contraband bathroom scissors.

"Janet," she replies.

"That's almost the same as your name."

"I know. It's silly."

"Heidi should be called Jane to keep with the pattern," I say. "Or maybe she should be called Theodora, after your dad."

Janna has a wide-open face like a snowy mountain top, a high porcelain forehead, and enormous blue eyes. "I wish my name was Stephanie," she confides, sorting through a stack of plastic armor.

"You know who your mom reminds me of a little?"

Janna shakes her head. "Who?"

"Janice. You know—Janice the Muppet." Janice had straight blond hair and big puffy lips and eyes that were always half-closed, like it hurt to look at things.

Now Janna's snowy white face is melting. "You think my mom looks like a Muppet?"

"It's not a bad thing," I reassure her. "But she does sort of look like Janice." As I thought about it, Janice the Muppet smiled a lot more, though.

When I glance up, Mrs. Lennox is leaning in the doorway, a dish towel on her shoulder, a sharp rent in the space between her brows.

A few weeks later, I am watching *The Muppet Show.* Janice is strumming her guitar and shaking her high blond ponytail, and I tap my father on the knee, enlist his opinion. "Dad, does Janice the Muppet remind you of anyone?"

"Person or Muppet?" he asks. He is always willing to play.

"Person."

"Child or grown-up?"

"Grown-up."

Just then, my mother walks in. She is wearing a red, checkered jacket and clip-on earrings cut in strange, geometrical designs. "It's Bingo tonight, so I'll be late," she announces.

We are barely listening. "Is it someone we know from church?" he inquires.

"Nope."

"What are you talking about?" My mother blocks the television and demands an answer.

"Julie says someone we know looks like Janice the Muppet."

"Don't be absurd. People can't look like Muppets," my mother replies.

"Mrs. Lennox does!" I retort, then instantly regret it.

My father laughs so his belly shakes, but my mother chides, "Bill, don't encourage this! Though—speaking of Janet Lennox—I have something horrible to tell you."

My ears perk up. "Not *you,*" my mother says, "your father. Go brush your teeth."

"But we're still eating dessert!"

I watch her lips contort like lava about to overflow the volcano of her mouth and decide to do as she says. Out of sight at the top of the stairs, I crouch down, silent as a good sleuth, and listen.

"Julie has a point," my father says, still chuckling.

"Julie has a sweet tooth and a wild imagination"—there is a pause in which I do my best not to breathe—"but Janet Lennox has a *boyfriend.*"

"What?"

"It's true. She's gotten herself involved with Tom, her rowing instructor. Too much time on her hands, and now too much time with a well-muscled man . . . I told her to join the Garden Club, but it's clear in retrospect that she had other plans."

"Is this just some rumor that you women—"

"It has been *verified* by Diane Saunders. Janet Lennox told her herself."

"But by boyfriend do you mean—"

"*Yes I mean*—three times a week—at her own house for all we know."

"Good Jesus," my father sighs. "What about Ted?"

"What *about* Ted? That's a good question."

"Does he know?"

"If he does, he's not likely to do anything about it. He'll just let it drag on until one of the girls walks in on them *exercising* in the middle of the living room."

"I did notice recently that she looks more fit."

"Bill, if you're not going to take this seriously, I don't think there's any point in talking to you about it." My mother's keys jingle, and I retreat as fast as I can down the upstairs hall.

Janna's sister Heidi is one of the popular girls. Two grades ahead of us and elegant like a willow tree that never gets rattled in wind, Heidi always has someone to talk to on the playground. She never walks the perimeter on her own kicking pebbles or leans against the fence gazing off into the distance, lonely and longing to be anywhere else. It is hard to know where my admiration of Heidi ends and my resentment of Heidi begins.

"See those kids on the track," Janna says, gesturing across the street and down to the adjacent field.

"Sure—from the high school."

"Well, I think one of them's my long-lost sister. Her name is Jessica, and her favorite color is purple. My parents gave her up for adoption because she was born when they were too young to take care of her."

I don't need any instruction in how to play make-believe. "Which one is she?" I ask, stuffing my toes into the fence holes.

"There!" Janna exclaims, as a dark-complected girl with long, wavy hair turns the corner and takes the baton. "That's Jessica!"

I climb up a few squares on the cyclone fence, and then I hear the whistle. When I glance behind me, Mrs. Reid and Mrs. Blankenship are shaking their heads and frowning.

"She seems like a good sister," I say. "You should write her a letter."

Soon, it is the end of the day, and we stand together on the yellow line waiting for our mothers to retrieve us. Mine is always late, so I have time to contemplate the slow progression of cars through the gate that our teachers strain to pull back on both sides.

Today Mrs. Lennox is leader of the shiny-bumpered pack of minivans and station wagons.

"Your mom looks different," I say as she strolls toward us, purse stretched bandolier-style across her chest. Mrs. Lennox's hair, which has always been a light honey color—what my mother calls "dirty blond"—is suddenly Highlighter-yellow, Crayola-yellow, like if you touched her, some of that yellow would rub off on your hands.

Janna shrugs. "She says it's the color it used to be when she was my age."

"Hello, Mrs. Lennox," I grin. "Your hair looks golden like a fairy princess."

She seems to be studying me, but through her dark glasses, I can't make out her eyes. "C'mon, Heidi, Janna," she beckons. "We have a lot to do before your father gets home."

At the dinner table, my mother and father pretend I cannot hear them, even though I'm sitting inches away.

"Did you hear that Ted bought Janet a bigger diamond?"

"Bigger? At the rate they're going, he should have taken the old one away."

"He *must* know," my mother sighs, dipping her pork in apple sauce, "but it's plain to see he's never going to confront her about it."

"Mrs. Lennox's hair is bright yellow now," I tell them. "It's so bright it almost hurts to look at her."

"Julie, just so we're clear," my father begins, "it isn't good manners to talk about other people behind their backs. We can do it because we're a family, but you should never have a conversation like this with your friends at school. Understand?"

I nod and choreograph a new dance of peas across my plate.

"Dyeing her hair," my mother remarks. "Let the mid-life crisis begin."

What of the boxes of L'Oreal permanent color she stows in her bathroom drawer? What of the day my cousin asked me, "Why is your mother's hair turning red when it always used to be brown?"

The next time I see Mrs. Lennox, Janna and I are playing with a Pogo ball on her long, sloped driveway bordered by a high rockery on either side. Heidi is sitting on the front porch painting her nails, and Mr. Lennox is trimming the parking strip with a contraption all the fathers reverently refer to as "an edger." It has a tall, wooden handle like a broomstick and a revolving, silver spike on the bottom that cuts a sharp line between the grass and the curb.

Mrs. Lennox honks at us to get out of the way. When we don't do it fast enough, she lays on the horn and makes thrashing motions with her hand.

"Janna, come unload these groceries! I'm already late for tennis as it is." When Mrs. Lennox steps out of the shade, an involuntary shriek escapes my lips.

"What is it?" she snaps. "What's with you?"

"Nothing." I shake my head but stand mesmerized beside the rockery, staring.

"Ted, there's a frozen pizza in here for dinner. You can read directions, right? You know how to turn on the oven?"

Mr. Lennox and I are both staring, and both of us are afraid to speak or look sideways.

Later, when everyone but Heidi has gone inside, I climb the stairs and muster the courage to tap on her knee.

"Yeah?"

"Heidi," I whisper. "Why is your mother orange?"

"That's not orange," Heidi says. "That's *tan*."

"How did it happen to her?"

"In a tanning bed, Stupid—how do you think?"

In the car on the way to swim lessons, I confide in my father. "Remember how you said it's OK to talk about someone if you're talking about them to a member of your own family?"

"Sure." He turns down the radio, but I can tell he is only listening to me with one ear.

"Well, it's about Mrs. Lennox."

My father punches the button, and suddenly everything is quiet. "Did you see something at their house?"

"Yes," I reply. "I saw Mrs. Lennox, and she looks like a creepy swamp monster. Her hair is bright yellow as a bale of hay, and her skin is bright orange like"—I look around for something to compare it to—"like a traffic cone or a crossing guard's jacket." It may be a slight exaggeration, but I need to convey the gravity of the situation.

He sighs. "Well, sometimes people decide to try to improve on what God gave them. And sometimes they learn the hard way that God made us best as we are."

"So, what about Mom?" I ask, because I know he is relaxed, his body unclenched, his posture always improved outside her presence.

"What about Mom?"

"She wears a lot of makeup and perfume, and I know she likes to color her hair." At this revelation, my father looks stricken, pulls over near a stranger's parking strip.

"How do you know about that?"

"Hair-color boxes," I say. "I always see the stained gloves and empty bottles in the trash, and there's a certain rotten-egg smell that goes along with those."

Now his hands are tensing up, and I stare at the black hairs on his knuckles, sorry to have broached the subject after all.

"Julie, what your mother does is just—it's *touching up*. There's a fine line between making the most of what you have and trying to be something else entirely. Your mother is happy with who she is, but Mrs. Lennox—with all this *dramatic* change—seems to be sending a different message."

"Why wouldn't she be happy?"

My father offers me a Cert breath mint from his secret stash, which is how I know the serious part of our conversation is coming to a close. "It's hard to tell, Julie. It's hard to tell what's going on with other people. And it's most important to let Mrs. Lennox work it out with God and with her family. No outside interference, OK?"

"OK," I say, but just to be safe, I keep one set of fingers crossed behind my back.

"OK. Good girl!" He pats my knee and makes a cautious return to traffic.

Most of the mothers come into the locker room at the Southwest Community Center. Today, since I am motherless, I stand in the corner, my colorful towel draped around me like a circus tent, too shy to undress in front of others.

"Are you ready?" Janna asks. She is already suited, all on her own. Mrs. Lennox braids Heidi's hair before the mirror.

"Just about," I say. "You can go ahead to the showers without me."

As I tuck my socks inside my shoes and fold my clothes so they fit back inside my bag, I can't help but study Mrs. Lennox in the bathroom mirror. She is humming softly, and the edges of her mouth seem less downturned than before—less of a grimace and more of a plain line of separable skin. Maybe my father was wrong. Maybe sadness wasn't always the cause of transformation. Her arms, bright as street signs under the fuzzy, fluorescent light, now have long ropes rippling under the surface, and the little pockets of wrinkled skin around her elbows—the ones every mother has—pull taut to disappearing with each comb-through of Heidi's hair.

"Do you need something?" Mrs. Lennox asks at last, meeting my eyes in the glass.

I shake my head. If I did, I knew I hadn't learned the words for it yet.

Janna tells me her long-lost sister Jessica is more than just a track star; she's also in a young astronaut training program at the high school. "In a few years, she'll be off to outer space, and then my parents will be really sorry."

"Do you think they miss her?"

"Not my mom so much, but I'm sure my dad does. He'd never say it, but sometimes he looks so sad"—the word for this, I want to tell her, is *forlorn*—"that he just sits in his chair all night and says nothing."

"Maybe he should go after her, ask for her back."

Janna is reluctant to admit I have a good idea. She lines up little stones along the fence post. "It isn't that easy. Jessica would have to want to come back, and she doesn't even know about us."

"What about my letter idea? Even if she doesn't write back, at least you would have told her how you feel."

Janna considers climbing up on the fence until she remembers we are under surveillance by the playground patrol. "I could write her a letter, I guess. I'd just have to make sure she gets it before she sets off for the moon."

Today my mother is talking on the phone with one of the other mothers. I can only be sure it isn't Mrs. Lennox because she murmurs the name Janet in those low tones she would never use to address the person herself. With her conversation in progress, my mother rummages inside the refrigerator, oblivious to my presence on the threshold, half-obscured behind the open basement door.

"So, you're sure Ted knows? And he's just what—going to let this run its course?"

I debate about going into her bedroom and picking up the other receiver.

"Oh, come on!" my mother exclaims in her most incredulous tone. "There's a difference between *in shape* and *wizened* like a— like, I don't even know what."

I decide it isn't worth the risk of moving, so I stand transfixed, my sticky feet on the slippery plastic runner.

"Patience is only a virtue sometimes," she snaps. "Seriously. Would she put up with it if the tides were turned—" I hear her laugh and open the cupboard. "Well, I guess the hard-body part wouldn't be so bad, but let's remember who we're talking about. She's a *mother* after all . . . Oh, I know. The big white sunglasses like Jackie O. It's like something out of a cartoon, or a tabloid. She's . . . exactly right—a *caricature* of her former self."

Janice the Muppet, I repeat inside my head.

"Well, all I can say is, if she doesn't get her act together soon, those girls are going to go by the wayside."

The long cord retracts toward the wall, so I step into the kitchen as if I have just arrived. My mother gestures for me to get my slippers, and when I return, she has already hung up the phone.

"Put an apron on," she instructs tersely. "Then come over here and help me pound the meat."

I study her elbows below her rolled-up sleeves, her thick forearms and solid wrists, her pale skin with its stippling of freckles. I can't say—I don't know how to say—but my stomach churns a little, and my palms turn moist, and I wish there was a way to avoid growing into a body, a person, a future exactly like this.

"Did your mom bring you today?" I ask Janna in the locker room.

"No—my dad." She looks puffy around the eyes and tired.

"Did you write to Jessica yet?"

"Not yet. My parents have been fighting a lot, and I've been listening."

"What are they fighting about?" I try to sound casual, like I can't imagine, even though I sense a fragile situation, a teacup dangling from a loosened nail.

"My mom's paying a ton of money to have her teeth whitened," Janna says. "It costs hundreds of dollars for every tooth you have done, and she wants to do all the teeth you can see."

"How many is that?" I ask.

"More than a thousand dollars, which my dad says is out of the question. But she says she'll do it anyway, one tooth at a time, and if he won't pay, she knows someone who will."

We stand in the shower together, soak up the wet and steam, then tug on our bathing suits and watch them puff out like pregnant bellies.

NO RUNNING, the sign reads, but we pretend not to see and leap into the water before the lifeguard's high-pitched whistle and megaphone chide.

A few weeks in the future, I make an almost-perfect dive after a series of unfortunate flops that turn my belly pink and tender. I look around in my elation, but this time no one is watching. I see a huddle of mothers on the bleachers, though my own mother is not among them. Then, off to the side, out of sight of the women, I see Ted, and I imagine—or perhaps it really occurs—that he nods at me, a nod of affirmation.

Gary, our swim teacher, tells us we are going to play shark tag, and as luck would have it, I am one of the first ones out. I pick up my towel and slip on my jelly shoes and look up at the mothers one last time. I have a sudden hunch that I am never going to be one of them—a mother, that is—and this premonition surprises me, but it doesn't makes me sad.

Slowly, I wander over to where Ted is waiting. "Hello, Mr. Lennox," I say.

This time I know for certain that he nods—the shy man's version of *hello*—and he doesn't seem to mind me standing there beside him. Janna is still in the game, so we watch her together and clap when she makes it safely to the wall.

"I brought Janna one of these—you know, cheese-and-cracker packs," he murmurs. "Would you like one, too? I have three."

I nod eagerly, and he deposits the coveted Handi-snack into my hands.

"These are the unsung treasure of the vending machines," I tell him. "Thank you."

He looks down at me, moves to pat my head but doesn't, and then I see that there are tears in his eyes. I realize that, in his own quiet way, Ted Lennox is crying in public.

Since I don't know what to say or do, and since my heart is fluttering with fear that something horrible is about to happen, I look down at the ground. I count cracks in the ancient floor. Then, I notice Mr. Lennox's big man-shoe is untied—a brown loafer of some kind, with a thick heel—and I bend down to tie it. I figure this is the least I can do.

When Janna wins the game, she comes rushing over, sliding on the slick concrete but not caring. "I won! I won!" she exclaims. "Gary says I get my pick of any candy I want!"

We are about to follow her to the ceremonious claiming of her prize when, to everyone's surprise, Mrs. Lennox appears.

"Oh dear," Ted says, and it isn't clear whether he means it as a greeting or an expression of dismay. "Was it not my turn to pick up Janna?"

"Mom, I won shark tag!" Janna proclaims.

"I took Heidi to the nail salon, and we got done early," Mrs. Lennox replies. I follow her eyes, but they do not settle on anyone in particular.

"Mom!" Janna tugs on Janet's tight blue jeans. "I won!"

"Good," she replies. "That's good. Go get your things together."

"I'll go with you—for the prize." Ted swaddles his daughter in a Garfield towel.

"I like your sandals," I tell Mrs. Lennox, who is standing beside me and a little apart, tall and slender, elegant in profile.

"Thank you," she says, aloof still but not unkind. Her toenails gleam bright red, her hair bright yellow, and her arms bright orange. She makes me think of Oz, a prism of pulsing light, the way Dorothy opens the door after the cyclone strikes and the whole world overwhelms her, intense and bewildering. Mrs. Lennox could be Janice the Muppet, or she could be the tallest mayor ever of Munchkinland.

"Do you need a ride home?" she asks, and when she turns to look at me, I see her two front teeth are glowing—the most luminous white I could imagine—as if she had covered over a mistake with Liquid Paper.

"No, thanks," I say. "My mother is coming. She's always a little bit late."

And though I can't be sure, I think Mrs. Lennox was smiling. I think she was standing there, staring out at the empty pool, the open space, watching the chlorine clouds waft away like ghosts. I hope she was thinking of her husband then, or of her daughter. Likely of Heidi, maybe of Janna—or maybe of the one on the moon.

Mrs. Newport

[Or a Study of Jealousy as a Blue-Eyed Monster]

Mrs. Newport was the mother of Devon Newport, the first boy my mother mused might be my knight in shining armor. Or, in this case, my knight in gray corduroy pants and two-tone tees. She liked the fact he never wore jeans.

"But I'm only seven," I protest, after my mother sees the seat assignments at Open House and discovers Devon and I have been paired for a three-week cycle.

"Miss Campbell says you get along well together." I am coloring at the kitchen table, and she is clipping coupons from the paper.

"I guess. He shares his eraser and isn't as gross as the other boys"—thinking of Carl Lull and the playground belching contests. Mostly, though, I am jealous I have never been asked to join.

"Do you ever imagine what it might be like to be Julie *Newport?*" my mother asks, putting her scissors down and smiling.

I'm still trying to imagine what it's like to be Julie Wade.

"When I was your age, we used to write down all the boys we liked and then try on each of their names. It was fun. It was like trying on a new outfit."

She never remembers that I don't like trying on clothes.

"Here." My mother takes a crayon—magenta or mulberry—and writes it for me: "*Julie Marie Newport*. Has a nice ring to it, wouldn't you say?"

I have told my mother that because I am in first grade, boys don't interest me much—they couldn't possibly. I'm too young. But the fact is, I have no short attention span when it comes to Chelsea Brothers, a sixth-grade girl with red curls and pink glasses and the best kickball kick around. I know I shouldn't be watching. I know my heart shouldn't rattle my chest like an old canteen, then charge up my throat like hungry soldiers storming a mess hall in the movies my father watches on TV. But something happens to me when we're waiting for our turn on the field, and the older kids walk past in their more efficient lines, talking easily with each other as if they have nothing to hide. I see Chelsea, and she is smiling at someone so the freckles bunch up on her nose, and suddenly I forget where I am, forget what I'm supposed to be doing. I forget everything until Simon Says or until the whistle blows.

My mother has arranged to have herself invited for tea at Mrs. Newport's house. I will come along and play with Devon and perhaps with his older sister, Renee.

"I've been dying to get inside that house," I hear my mother say. "She's just so smug about it—as if Genesee Hill is the new hot spot in town and Fauntlee Hills is some kind of slum."

"I doubt she thinks that," my father replies.

"It's this whole married-to-a-doctor business that gets me. Fine— he's a doctor—but an *ophthalmologist*. The way she struts around, you'd think he was a brain surgeon."

To be fair, I have never seen Mrs. Newport strut. Strutting is for peacocks and other exotic birds. Mrs. Newport moves slowly, with predicated grace. She has long, thin fingers and gentle hands that she is good about laying on your shoulder when she asks you a question. I love her soothing voice and her glossy clear nails and her signature sweaters, which are light in color and always have a bright blouse with a starched collar beneath them. She wears little gold hoops in her ears, and a little gold band on her finger, and I can't imagine she ever gets angry or dirty, and her skin always smells like a fresh peach.

"Remember to be on your best behavior," my mother instructs. "Imagine the Newports as your future in-laws."

"I don't know what that means."

"Look everyone in the face and don't eat too much when snacks are offered."

We ring the doorbell and stand pushing our spines straighter and straighter, my mother in her broomstick skirt and turquoise blouse, my hair pulled back and braided through with ribbon.

The Newport house has high ceilings and hardwood floors and a kitchen with an island that stretches almost to the living room. It is open and spacious like houses I have seen in magazines, with windows cut out of the roof and the occasional step up or step down that doesn't belong to a flight of stairs. The white sofa curves around the corner like a cat's flexible back, and the bookcases are built into the walls and covered with glass.

"Welcome!" Mrs. Newport smiles. She wears lavender slacks to match the lavender blouse beneath her gray cashmere sweater. "Devon and Renee have just returned from ice-skating lessons, so they'll be down as soon as they've had their showers. The tea is steeping, Linda, and in the meantime"—she lays a hand on my shoulder and bends toward me so as not to tower—"what would you like to drink?"

I glance at my mother, then reply. "Nothing just yet, thank you. I'll wait to see what Devon is thirsty for."

"All right, then. Shall I give you the tour? Would you like to see the rest of our little cottage?"

I am about to observe that this isn't a cottage at all—more like a mansion or perhaps a chateau, though I am less certain of the latter word's requirements. My mother pinches my arm, intercepts me quickly: "Yes, of course, Beth. We'd love to."

Later, Devon and I recede to his room, drinking Hi-Cs and finding we have less to say to each other outside of school.

"Do you have any pets?" I ask, following his example and sitting cross-legged on the plush blue carpet.

"We used to have a cat named Daisy, but she ran away when we moved."

"Oh," I nod, sipping the juice while my eyes wander the length of the walls. "Our mailman has a daughter named Daisy and another daughter named Lily. I always think it's funny that cats can have people names."

"People can have flower names," he remarks, "so I guess cats can, too."

This observation makes me smile, and I wonder if Devon Newport is one of those "still waters that run deep," an expression I have heard my father use before. In fact, Devon looks a little like pictures I've seen of my father as a child—a gap between his new front teeth, a handful of freckles garnishing his cheeks, and blondish-red hair cut close to his scalp with bangs that resemble a girl's. Devon is also "tall and husky," in my mother's words, and she has mentioned before that he looks like he'll be "a natural on the football field."

"So, do you play sports or anything?" I inquire.

"Yeah," he says. "I'm an ice-skater."

"That isn't a real sport—is it?"

"Sure, it is. Didn't you see the Winter Games?" I shrug. "The ones in Japan?" I tug on my straw, thinking. "Well, you've seen figure skating before, right?"

"I guess so."

"Who do you think holds the women up? The men have to be really strong." Devon turns emotional now, twisting his hands as he explains.

I nod. "That makes sense."

"Do you want to go out back and play on my swing set?"

Devon Newport is so lucky. Imagine having a swing set and *a sister.*

When he opens the closet to find his shoes, I notice the top shelf is covered with Care Bears. From my vantage, it seems there must be more than a dozen of them, all crammed together, a few even upside down.

"I love Care Bears," I say. "I only have one, though. The one with the rainbow on her belly."

Now Devon's face turns the color of bologna before the cream cheese, and he slams the door shut in a hurry. "You aren't supposed to see those."

"Why not?"

"Just"—he paces now, nervously, the perimeter of the room—"my mother doesn't want anyone to know I have them."

"Are they hand-me-downs from your sister or something?"

Devon is a bad liar. He looks to the side, then away as he answers, "Yeah. They're mostly all Renee's."

At home, my mother serves French dip sandwiches, which we don't often have, which makes me wonder if we're celebrating some kind of victory.

"Did you have fun, Smidge?" my father asks, covering his tie with a napkin.

"It was OK," I say. I want to tell him about the Care Bears but sense I shouldn't, sense it will put them both in mind of Steven Mann and my own past playing with the wrong sorts of toys.

"The house is nice—if you like that kind of floor plan," my mother concedes. "It's clear his practice must be doing well."

"Devon and Renee take ice-skating lessons," I say. "I thought ice-skating was only for girls." This is how I test the waters.

"I used to ice-skate when I was a boy," my father replies, "but there weren't any lessons. What's to learn? You go down to the lake, put on some skates, and have a go at it." Of course my father is from Montana, where it was always easy to find a frozen lake in winter.

"They skate at an indoor rink—like roller-skating, but with blades instead of wheels."

"Isn't that kind of nancy?" my father asks, raising his eyebrows at my mother.

"Bill, trust me. Devon Newport is 100 percent boy. He's probably just doing it so Renee will have someone to go with." Now my mother turns a diligent eye in my direction. "You know, it wouldn't hurt you to try some ice-skating lessons. I think it helps with posture and balance, and coupled with ballet . . ."

Her voice trails off, and I know she is suggesting something I don't quite understand. I imagine it has to do with the awkwardness I feel in my own body, the shame that falls over my face each time the other girls sink down into splits while I sit high and straining with my long, inflexible limbs.

"Did you see Henry?" My father's voice is hushed, as if hoping I won't hear.

"No. He was at the office, I guess, but I did think about your sister while I was there."

Now I am listening more keenly than ever. "What about Aunt Linda?" I want to know.

My parents exchange a furtive glance. "Well," my father says at last. "Your Aunt Linda went to high school with Henry Newport. They were in the same class."

"Was he her boyfriend?" I ask.

"They were just friends," my mother replies, a little too fast, a little too eager to change the subject. "Now make sure to eat some of your salad."

The next year in school, we have a man-teacher, and I try to keep an open mind about it. After all, if Devon Newport can ice-skate and collect Care Bears, Mr. Whited should be able to teach if he wants to. On his desk, he keeps pictures of his daughters, and sometimes his wife brings him lunch in a Tupperware container he heats up in the communal microwave. Although he seems nice on the surface,

Mr. Whited also has a dark side, a temper that stretches out like seaweed and tangles your legs as you try to swim past. As with my mother, you don't want to make him mad.

Lana Steeley must not realize she is taking her life in her hands—all eight years of meticulous self-construction—when she passes the note to Erin Saunders during Language Arts time. I watch the sheet of blue-striped notebook paper slide from palm to palm, listen for the crinkle as Erin unfolds the top, the sides, the little isosceles of secret. Then, suddenly, Mr. Whited is upon her, seizing the note in his huge white hands, holding it up like a victory flag.

"Well, well, let's see what we have here—" in the slow, detestable tone of a movie villain. "Isn't this interesting?" He turns the paper around so the whole class can see. It is a blue-ink drawing of a bed with tall posts and two heads propped on pillows. "The caption reads—" He is taking his time to increase the suspense, to heighten Lana's pink-faced horror. I wonder if the lights will flicker, with Mr. Whited soon found slumped on the floor. "—Lana and Lee, naked in bed." Gasps and giggles from around the room. "So, this is a pic-ture—in case we weren't sure—of Lana Steeley" (pointing to the girl-head with pigtails and bows) "and Lee Magnussen" (pointing to the boy-head with spiky hair) "NAKED in BED."

Why would they be naked? I wondered. *Had there been a fire? Had something happened to their clothes?*

"Where are you in this, Erin? Are you taking a Polaroid picture?"

"I didn't know what was in it," she says, her hands retracting into the sinkholes of her sleeves.

"Lee, it looks like you have a not-so-secret admirer," Mr. Whited proclaims, carrying the note across the room and placing it dramati-cally on the desk of the boy beside me. "If I were you, I'd have this picture framed, hang it up on your bedroom wall like a pennant."

Lee's face doesn't flush, and his hands don't tremble. He keeps his eyes firmly glued to the floor.

"As for Miss Steeley, she and her friend Miss Saunders are going to spend today's recess cleaning out the rabbit cage. And tomor-row's recess. And recess the day after that."

I look over at Lana, whose small face is wide and red as a camellia, whose eyes have pooled into two small puddles of tears.

"And if I catch anyone else passing notes in class, you'll have to stand up and kiss the subject of your note in front of everyone." More gasps and giggles. "*Then,* you'll have to clean the rabbit cage."

By second-grade standards, this is a scandal. I want to tell someone, but I have to be careful in whom I choose to confide.

"Shall we go outside and practice our jacks?" Aunt Linda suggests. She is teaching me the game with the little red ball and the strange silver pieces that look like you could fold them together into miniature jungle gyms. On my grandmother's driveway, we sit down and savor the early spring sun.

"I have a question," I say, after I'm sure we won't be overheard.

"OK. I hope I have an answer." Her hair is feathered and frosted creamy-gold like Farrah Fawcett's, the way my mother says has "long since gone out of fashion." I think the style looks pretty on her, though. Soon, Aunt Linda pulls her sunglasses out of her hair and slips them over her nose, which means I won't be able to scan her eyes, assess the truth of any response she gives me.

I want to say what happened, to simply recount events, but I sense I will need to ease more slowly into this subject—like using the ladder in a swimming pool instead of leaping off the ledge. "Well, it's about boys," I begin. "How do you know if you like a boy?"

"I guess you want to spend time with him. You watch for him, and you notice when he's not there."

"What if you're *glad* he's not there?"

Aunt Linda laughs now and stretches her legs in the track pants that crinkle like tissue paper. "Then, I guess you don't like him very much. Or—maybe you feel shy because you *do* like him, and you're relieved that you don't have to try so hard that day."

"And how do you know if a boy likes you?" This is a good strategy, I think, because soon I will reveal that I'm asking on behalf of Lana Steeley who got caught drawing naughty pictures in class. Maybe she was trying to get Lee to like her.

"Someday, if they like you, boys will be able to tell you to your face. It's harder now because they're still figuring out who they are." This is a feeling I understand so well that I am filled with sudden compassion for boys.

"So, why don't girls just tell them—to their faces—if they know?" This is important. This is going to be my seamless segue to Lana Steeley.

"It's not very ladylike," Aunt Linda sighs. "It's better to let the boy make the first move."

What I mean to say is how Lana Steeley might have wanted Lee Magnussen to like her, but since she couldn't tell him to his face, she had to find another way—embarrassing, yes, but undeniably certain, a spilled secret maybe worth the rabbit cage. Instead, out of nowhere: "Did you like Mr. Newport in high school? Did Mr. Newport like you?"

The jacks scatter from Aunt Linda's hand. "Mr. Newport?"

"Henry Newport, Devon Newport's dad."

"Where did you hear about that?" she asks, folding her long fingers into awkward shapes.

"Nowhere. I mean, you just hear things. Did he ask you to a dance? Did you ever pass notes about him in class?"

"No." She shakes her head, fiddles with her zipper so I won't see the pink splotches forming on her throat. "Nothing like that. People can know each other—they can be acquaintances without—" The little red ball lodges in the grass. "Always remember," she says, "not every story is a love story. Most stories are anything but."

I decide to make a list of every kind of story I know. There are love stories of course, and fairy tales, and murder mysteries, and other kinds of mysteries where no one dies. *Is that it? Is that everything?* I twist my brain into knots, tighter than snarled hair or too-small sweaters, but I can't come up with anything else.

In third grade, we study cursive writing. Once we've learned to make all our letters by tracing along in the workbook, Mrs. Moak distributes large sheets of paper with a blank space on top and lines like train tracks passing through the middle of the page.

"Today," she says, "you're going to write a story. You can write anything you want, but you have to use cursive letters. When you're finished writing, you can draw a picture to illustrate your work."

Devon Newport is once again my random-assignment seatmate. In quiet defiance of the rules, he takes out his Crayola kit and begins his picture-making first. In the far-left corner, he draws a tall brown building with lots of windows and a sign on the lawn. In the far-right corner, he draws a house with a chimney puffing smoke and a circular driveway with a car parked close to the house.

"Julie, eyes on your own paper!" Mrs. Moak commands.

"What story are you going to write?" I ask Devon, sharpening my pencil with protracted care.

"I'm writing a true story," he replies. "It's about my family and how we have to live in a hotel until they finish construction on our house."

"You're living in a hotel?" I whisper, incredulous.

"Uh-huh. My mom says it will take at least two whole months to finish the master bedroom and the rooftop terrace."

I glance at his paper and notice a large round of blue in the center. "Is that a lake?" I ask.

"No. That's the swimming pool my parents are putting in the backyard."

This information is too much for me to contain. At the dinner table, almost before my father has finished saying grace, I burst out, "The Newports are going to have a swimming pool in their back-yard!"

"Well, you have a swimming pool," my father replies, "though I guess you've all but outgrown it by now."

"Not that kind of swimming pool," I say. "Devon told me all about it. They're living in a hotel, and they have bulldozers digging up their backyard and everything. The pool is going to be built into the ground like the one at Southwest Community Center. They're even going to have a hot tub and an outdoor shower."

My mother's eyes narrow, and she inspects my face for any trace of insincerity. "This sounds like a whale of a tale to me," she replies.

"Call Mrs. Newport," I challenge. "See for yourself."

My mother regards me a moment, then her corn on the cob, then the knife in her hand, still aimed at the margarine stick. Finally, having made her decision, she stands up, strides over to the phone, and dials a number. "If you're lying to me, there *will* be consequences."

I fidget in my chair while my father puts down his fork and happily peruses the paper. He knows he's not allowed to read during meals, but my mother's absence from the table constitutes a brief intermission.

"Beth?"—a pause, and then, on a note of moral indignation—"Figures *they* would have an answering machine."

As she listens, my mother jots down a number on one of her recipe cards, then returns to the table, a troubled expression on her face. "It seems the Newports have, in fact, *temporarily relocated* to the Holiday Inn. Here's the number where they can be reached," she says, waving the card like a fan and frowning.

I smile and rock in my chair. "See? I told you! Devon lives in a hotel now. They're getting a swimming pool. It's a true story!"

Not only is this story true, but for some reason, it is especially upsetting to my mother. When I bring home the invitation to our end-of-year party, she takes it from me and crumples the yellow paper masterfully stenciled with beach balls and picnic baskets. The invitation reads: *Come join us for a celebration of your child's successful completion of third grade. This year's party will be hosted by the Newport family. Students should bring swimsuits, towels, and a change of clothes, as it will be a swimming party. Parents are requested to contribute a side dish or dessert.*

Later that night, propped on my lacy pillows, I commence reading a Crowell biography of an important woman named Jane Addams. This new genre of true stories is what we have been assigned to read for our first-ever *oral* book reports. Mrs. Moak helped us each select a historical figure she thought we'd admire. In addition to reading and writing about the person in question, we are required to stand before our peers and present what we have learned to the class.

"You know I've always wanted a swimming pool," my mother snaps, slamming the basement door and loudly securing the lock.

"You can still have one," my father assures her. "It's not like there's a limit on the number of pools or a shortage of people to hire."

I climb out of bed and move quickly to the threshold of my room, listening as their conversation unfolds.

"But now it's *ruined,* Bill. Don't you see? It's not our special thing anymore. It's the Newports.' Why is it always the Newports?"

"I don't think—"

"Beth Newport has never worked a day in her life, and here I am, doing the reading program, tutoring for the schools. You know that's what I wanted to do with the money." She is stomping her feet, which makes the chandelier in the dining room shake and the dishes in the cabinets wobble.

"No one's stopping you from doing it," my father replies. "Why are you making this a competition?"

"Oh, that's rich. *I'm* making it a competition. *I'm* bragging to everyone about how we just remodeled our house that we only bought two years ago." She starts to cry, and my father cannot console her, and before long she is calling him names and telling him *he* should go live at the Holiday Inn. This prospect pleases me, provided I can go with him.

"You know," I tell my Aunt Linda, "you remind me a lot of Jane Addams. She was a very nice person, and she liked to travel, and she never got married in her whole life. I'm not sure if she even had a boyfriend."

We are sitting at my grandmother's kitchen table, she with her cup of coffee, I with my glass of milk. Aunt Linda musters a wan smile, then glances at Grandma June, who is playing Solitaire and listening while we talk.

"Jane Addams received the Nobel Peace Prize," my grandmother says without looking up. "It's a remarkable honor, particularly for a woman."

"You were alive then, right, Grandma?"

"Yes, I was. I was about twenty years old, as I recall." She smiles at me, chews her dry toast contentedly.

"Did you *know* Jane Addams?" This possibility intrigues me, and I nearly catapult from my chair at the thought.

"No, no," she chuckles, "nothing like that. But I did know *of* her and of all the good work she did at Hull House."

The tight lines in Aunt Linda's cheeks have loosened now, and she suggests I practice my book report for them. "Be sure to read slowly and clearly and to pause now and then to look people in the eye."

I stand up, smooth the wrinkles from my paper, and commence with confidence: "Jane Addams was an important American woman born in 1860. She lived for 74 years but always had a lot of health problems. Her father encouraged her to go to college, even though this wasn't typical for women of her time. Not only did she go to college in the United States and Europe, but she also never got married or had any children, which would probably have made her father really sad if he hadn't dropped dead suddenly when she was still a young woman."

When I stop to breathe and make eye contact with the audience, I catch my aunt and grandma exchanging circumspect looks. "After that, Jane Addams inherited money and started having a lot more fun. She traveled with her stepmother and her college friend Ellen Starr, and throughout her life, she had a lot of lady friends who lived with her and helped her with her helping of others, especially Mary Rozet Smith, whom she seemed to like best of all."

My grandmother raises her hand, a gentle interruption of my speech. "You know, dear," she says, "I think you might not want to focus so much on Jane Addams' personal life. Your teacher likely wants to know why she was honored with the Nobel Peace Prize—what service she performed, what organizations she belonged to. It isn't really relevant whether she was married or how she spent her private time."

"But isn't that why she could do all the good things she did? Because she didn't have to cook dinner every night for her husband and change her children's dirty diapers all the time?" This is the hypothesis that has been forming in my mind—that if you want to be important as a woman, you might have to forgo the traditional path.

I think I see the faint curve of a smile pass over my Aunt Linda's lips, but she looks down at her crossword page and says nothing. My grandma's reply has the ring of stifled exasperation: "Well, every woman serves in her own way. Whatever else, you must remember that."

My mother has made tinker cake and sliced it into several dozen pieces. She has wound her hair with hot curlers, lifted hand weights in her bedroom, and put on a pair of white pants, gold thongs, and a Hawaiian shirt layered with large, wood beads. I wear my swimsuit under my clothes and wince as she pulls my hair back into a headache-inducing ponytail. Since I'm going to be playing in the water, she says, there's no point trying to make me look good; *decent* is the best we can do.

"Remember to be as gracious as possible to Mrs. Newport. Compliment her on the changes they've made to the house, especially the swimming pool. The last thing we want her to think is that you're jealous." Her eyes are blue as the tips of flames.

"Don't worry," I tell my mother. "I'm not jealous. I think it's too cold to have a swimming pool in Seattle anyway. A hot tub would be pretty nice, though."

When we arrive, Mrs. Newport greets us warmly, offers to take my bag and stow it away in Renee's room. "We have two bathrooms on the main level and another upstairs," she says, leaning in and addressing me directly. "You can change wherever you feel comfortable. And when you're ready, head right out to the pool."

"I *am* ready," I say, peeling off my shirt and shorts and handing them in earnest to my mother.

Mrs. Newport smiles, her cheeks the same color as her thin cardigan and matching slacks. It is the color I have heard my mother call *primrose* while studying swatches of paint.

"Well then, off with you!" she exclaims, gesturing toward the sliding glass doors.

"Oh, by the way," I call over my shoulder, imitating housewives I've heard on TV, "I love what you've done with the place!"

The swimming pool is shaped like a kidney bean with warm inlaid bricks around the edges and shiny blue tiles along the interior wall. The sides and bottom resemble a bathtub—toothy-white, almost like porcelain—though to the touch, the surface feels rough, nothing you could slip on but nothing sharp or jagged either. The hot tub curves into the pool on one side, with a slot in the blue-tiled wall where steamy water cascades in a constant waterfall. Soon, I have lost myself in a cannonball contest with Devon and some of the boys. When Mr. Newport comes home, it's time for hot dogs and hamburgers, which he cooks over the grill with his sleeves rolled up and his shiny blue tie still on.

"What do you tell Mr. Newport?" my mother nudges me from behind.

"Thank you—for the food and for letting us swim in your pool. It's really the best pool ever, even on a cloudy day."

He is shorter than my father, with darker hair, though I can see his sideburns have turned to salt and pepper. "It's our pleasure," Mr. Newport replies. "What's the good of having these little luxuries if you can't share them with other people?"

As my mother begins to inquire about length and depth and landscaping work and choice of tile, I wander into the house, looking for the cookies Mrs. Saunders is famous for. When I see Mrs. Moak, she hands me my report card and wishes me well in fourth grade. "You have a lot of spirit," she says. "Now it's time to work on harnessing your potential toward the most fruitful outcomes."

I nod, not sure what she means, and tear open the envelope—our first year of letter grades.

There is an A in Science, another in Math, another in History and Geography and Physical Education and—"Mrs. Moak?"

She turns back mid-bite, her bun dripping ketchup out the sides.

"How did I get a B+ in Language Arts class? Words are my favorite subject."

"You're good with language," she tells me, "and you have strong reading comprehension skills. But Language Arts also includes your penmanship and your book report, both of which"—she hesitates—"aren't quite up to snuff."

"What is snuff?" I plead. "Nobody ever told me what snuff is."

I feel the tingling sensation inside my nostrils, which means I am going to cry. "It's just an expression, dear," and Mrs. Moak's own expression softens. I have seen this look on my dance teacher's face, when I muddled the arabesque; on my ski instructor's face, when I missed the slalom gate. "It means—in both cases—you haven't learned how to follow the pattern *precisely* yet. You tend not to follow directions, even when they are very clearly given."

I pass the refrigerator on my way to the bathroom, the tears burning like too-hot cocoa inside.

Mrs. Newport has already put Devon's report card on display: seven perfect "A"s like arrows through the bull's eye of the page. Suddenly, a streak of anger—*or is it something else?*—preempts my sadness, bars the liquid heat from streaming from my eyes. No one sees me as I tear it down. I look around, expecting consequences, sure that someone will intercede.

Outside the adults are eating and chatting, and the children are playing in the pool. No one is watching as I climb the stairs—stealthily, taking two at a time. In the master bathroom, over the well-scrubbed toilet bowl, I shred our records, his and mine, then lean on the silver handle and flush with all my might.

Epilogue: Fourth Grade End-of-Year Party, Southgate Roller Rink

Devon Newport doesn't do so well on roller skates. It turns out wheels are harder for him than blades. Lee Magnussen and I have been skating together all afternoon, but now he's gone off with Marissa Sheldon in search of soda, and I can't find a trace of them near the concession stand.

When I slump down beside Devon on the brown carpeted bench, we nod at each other, affirm our mutual discontent, rub our skate-wheels on the rug and brood in silence.

Finally, he says, "I hear your parents put in a swimming pool."

"Yeah," I tell him, "it's true."

"I hear it looks just like ours. I mean, *exactly*. Down to the last detail. Down to the shape and size and the blue rim of tile."

There is no use denying anything: "Yeah. It's like they had a copy machine."

To my surprise, he doesn't get mad, doesn't pick up or scoot away: "Do you like it?"

"Well, it wasn't my idea in the first place, and to tell you the truth, I liked the grass a whole lot better."

Just then, Mrs. Newport steps through the doors, pushing them open like the passage to a pantry. Her hair gleams gold, then silver, beneath the disco-ball light, and she waves to Devon from a distance, motions that it's time to go.

"Don't tell my mom," he says. "It would hurt her feelings. But if I'm being honest"—he looks squirrely now, like before with the Care Bears—"I really miss my swing set sometimes."

Mrs. Fischer

[Or a Study of Minimalism with Natural and Synthetic Fibers]

It only took one glance at Alicia Fischer and a second glance at her mother to understand what people meant by the expression "cut from the same cloth." And because I was the kind of kid who spent a lot time thinking about expressions, I always tried to extend them to their literal ends.

For instance, both Alicia and Mrs. Fischer had smooth, dark hair of the sort popular in shampoo commercials. This hair was most often described in voiceover as "silky" or "silken," and silk, everyone knew, was a premium fabric. They also had pale white skin that was exceptionally soft to the touch—as soft as a cashmere sweater. When we passed such sweaters adorning mannequins in the mall, my mother would flick the price tag with her fingertip and scowl.

It wasn't that the Fischers were easy to look at, not exactly. Their features weren't so much lovely as severe. But once you started looking, you would find it hard not to notice: the style that set them apart, their *sophistication* I guess you could call it. That is, they had thin, polished lips, shiny as satin. Their skin pulled perfectly taut over their skeletons so nothing ever jiggled or seemed to come unhinged. And as it was with Alicia, so it was with her mother: a sharp, angular face, a small, pert nose, and cheekbones that rose out of the flesh like moons.

My own mother and I didn't share such a conspicuous family resemblance, but I had to admit I thought about the cloth. It was hard not to, especially after Alicia and I became friends. For instance, my mother and I had thick, coarse hair that turned to tulle in the heat or the rain, so a good portion of the time, we walked around with brown tutus on our heads.

Our skin was soft enough, I suppose, but flecked with freckles and moles, stenciled with tan lines, mosquito-bitten—we both had that sweet blood. In the summers, I cloaked myself in calamine lotion, and still my skin turned against me, a scratchy blanket I longed to remove.

Alicia didn't seem to have these problems. She and Mrs. Fischer were made of finer stuff—*organza, chiffon*—fabrics you couldn't find on the bargain rack or at the back of the grocery store. In fact, they liked to shop in places where you made appointments or had to ring a little bell. They were Nordstrom's to our Kmart, Pantene to our White Rain. They were matching pashminas with a subtle fringe. My mother and I were polyester people.

I met Alicia on the warm, late-summer day my friend Joy and I went blackberry-picking atop the steepest hill in our neighborhood—39th Avenue—walled with houses of increasing grandeur on either side and a dense thicket at the center crest that stretched well beyond our sightline. This was, at the time, the outer limit of the world we knew, as far as our parents would permit us to wander without a chaperone. We approached the summit reverently, voices ragged from the climb.

"How many blackberries do you think it takes to make a pie?" Joy asked, her beach pail dangling from her hand as she appraised the fragrant brambles before us.

"Let's be honest," I said. "Are we really here for the blackberries, or is that just our cover?"

Recently, Joy and I had started a dog-walking business with the understanding that this would give us unquestioned access to the yards of our neighbors. As budding sleuths, we prized access above almost everything else.

"I thought we were in it for the berries, but . . ." She pivoted on the heels of her navy dock shoes, opened her eyes parachute-wide. "What did you have in mind?"

"Well, it's just that—" I tipped my head in the direction I wanted her to look.

"Is there something wrong with your neck?" Joy was kind-hearted, but she could be dense as a blackberry thicket sometimes.

"No—*over there*," I whispered, leaning again toward the enticing flight of concrete stairs leading up and beyond our neighborhood.

"Oh, Julie, you know we're not supposed to."

"But think of all the blackberries," I coaxed her, winking. "We might have to climb a little higher if we want to pick enough for a pie."

Just then, we heard a door creak open and a creamy voice call out, "Is that you, Joy? What are you doing here?"

Busted! my inner critic shouted, then stopped to consider: *We haven't even done anything yet.*

"Alicia? Wow. I didn't know you lived so close. Did you move or something?"

Joy was walking then toward a tall, lithe girl in black leggings, her shirt bright white like she never spilled. She looked like a child model in her boatneck with three-quarter sleeves, the kind of girl my mother sighed over in catalogs, then groaned, "Think of the salaries those kids bring home. Think what a gift they are to their families."

"Yeah, we moved last year. My parents love this house because it sits up so high. We do have a terrific view."

I lingered in the background, dragging my generic tennis shoes (my mother said they were "made in the spirit of Keds") toe-down across the fractured pavement.

"Hey, this is my friend, Julie," Joy said. When she beckoned to me, I trotted eagerly forward and stuck out my hand the way my father taught me to do.

Alicia hesitated, looked to Joy for confirmation that I wasn't someone to be wary of despite my sweaty armpit circles and tutu hair.

"Julie is a great detective," Joy assured her. "She's definitely somebody you want to get to know."

Alicia pressed her well-lotioned palm into mine and smiled. "And Alicia," Joy grinned, "is the best dancer in our troupe, hands-down."

"You're just saying that." Alicia bowed her head like she was blushing, but no color surged through her ivory cheeks.

"Here's the thing," I told Alicia, feeling a new imperative to take charge of the situation, to prove myself a leader worth following. "We're picking blackberries to make a pie, but we've been thinking about going up The Stairs." Whenever Joy and I spoke of The Stairs, they were capitalized. Our hushed and solemn voices made it so. "Have you ever climbed The Stairs?"

Alicia looked past me in the direction my body bent. "You mean, right over there? Those stairs?"

Joy and I nodded in unison, breath sucked back in our throats.

"Sure. Dozens of times." She shrugged. "My morning carpool picks me up at the top of those stairs."

"What's up there?" My voice shifted from whisper to tremble, and Joy grabbed my wrist as if bracing herself for a quake.

"Oh, it's just another neighborhood—not really so different from this one."

"That's it? That's all?" I pressed.

"Well, there is some kind of meditation center." Alicia braided her hair seamlessly as she spoke. "You can't see it clearly because it's set back from the road, but the sign says something about the Buddha, and there's a picture of a lotus flower."

Joy and I clutched each other, gleaming. We were two prospectors who had struck sudden gold. Alicia turned out to be our metal detector.

Unfortunately, in the midst of the moment's paramount excitement, I tripped on my shoelaces and crashed face-first to the ground. My body smacked hard, with barely time to brace.

"Oh my gosh! Are you all right?" Alicia and Joy helped me stand, but already the gray slabs at my feet were speckled with bright red dots.

"What's bleeding?" Joy wanted to know. My bare arms and legs were scuffed, the new white lines turning pink like a sunset as blood began to surface in my wounds. But it was my nose—my already knobby and self-conscious nose—that gushed, a faucet that would not shut off.

"I'll be fine," I said, squeezing my nostrils closed as best I could. This was far from my first nosebleed or my first clumsy fall. "If someone could just get me a Kleenex, I'm ready for our big trip up The Stairs."

Alicia, who I had known less than five minutes and who, to be fair, had no idea how prone to mishap I was, rushed inside to get her mother. Soon, a woman in a crisp, white shirt with a perfect part in her hair—that little glimpse of scalp like light filtering through trees—crouched before me to inspect the damage. I observed that even the toes peeking out from her dark huaraches were painted to match her pants.

"I'm Margot Fischer," she said, as though making a public debut. "If you'll come this way, I can help you clean yourself up and bandage some of these cuts. Alicia, she'll need to borrow a shirt; hers is quite soiled." I looked down at my light cotton blouse, the eyelet pattern my mother had chosen to give me a more "delicate" look. Now the blood and dirt had commingled into a series of grimy spirals.

"I'm really fine," I protested, but she was already steering me toward the two-car garage.

"Alicia, please run inside and open the door." In a moment, we stepped through into the cool shade of the cleanest garage I had ever seen. There was no trace of yard debris, no row of dented cans, no pile of outdated magazines. A spotless Volvo station wagon occupied one side, and on the other—where another car should be—I looked for it but could not make out even the tiniest rainbow of oil.

Mrs. Fischer, with a magician's efficiency, produced wet wipes to eliminate my first layer of filth. She held me steady as I slipped my feet out of my shoes—a reverse Cinderella move—and then guided me inside to a place she called "the powder room." I looked around at the scalloped mirror, the pedestal sink, the toilet disguised beneath a fluffy beret, but there was no sign of powder or the puff.

"Here's tissue," she said, "for your nose. If you sit down and tip your head back, the bleeding will stop sooner. There are washcloths and such in the cupboard, so when you're all fresh, let me know, and I'll bring the Neosporin." Joy stood in the doorway, taking it all in. Alicia handed me a soft blue button-down made of some material I didn't recognize.

"Thanks," I say. "This is so pretty."

"It's linen," she replied like a knowing adult. "I find it very breathable."

When I was all clean, we reconvened in Alicia's room with homemade lemonade and ginger cookies. "Did your mother actually squeeze the lemons herself?" I asked. A fresh slice of lemon dangled from the side of my glass, pleasing as a crescent moon.

"Well, I helped her," Alicia said, adjusting the coiled neck of her lamp. She shined it beneficently toward a small cactus village arranged on a bed of rocks. "And sometimes our housekeeper helps a little in the kitchen, though she's mostly here for the drapes and the rugs."

Joy wanted to forego our sleuthing expedition until the next day after learning that Alicia had a Slip 'N Slide all set up on the most precarious slope of her lofty backyard. I wanted to get back to the business of The Stairs right after snack, but I, too, had grown distracted. *Was it possible the Fischers might prove just as mysterious as the Buddhist meditation center? More?*

"So, your mother doesn't work, but she still has a housekeeper?"

"No woman should have to do it all herself," Alicia replied.

"Are your parents art dealers?" I asked, thinking back on the enormous black vases in the entryway, the slender strands of bamboo, the calligraphy on canvas lining the white, imperial walls.

"Just collectors," she said. I envied Alicia her nonchalance, how she moved around the room like a much older girl, confident and at ease in her body. "My mother always says it's better to have a few nice things than a house full of junk."

I thought about my own mother then, of our dining room table's tidal waves of clutter: the crumpled grocery lists, the plastic sacks of unsatisfactory merchandise, the stack of receipts marked "to be returned," and the stack of rainchecks labeled "pick up soon." At home, our walls were thickly papered, which made the rooms feel small, stuffy. Our cabinets were crowded with Precious Moments figurines, and no tabletop was left without a centerpiece, sometimes two or three.

Even the wide picture windows facing Puget Sound had grown narrow, dotted with suction cups bearing an assortment of hooks. On these hooks, small panels of stained glass—a bouquet of roses, a pair of hands folded in prayer—fit awkwardly together like blocks in a Tetris game.

After some mulling: "I think your mother may be right," I said.

The next day, Joy and I trudged back up 39th Avenue to where Alicia stood, angel-radiant, in the afternoon light. We had told her, being a novice sleuth, to aim for incognito. She wore a sleeveless sheath embellished with green foliage. The fern fronds appeared to wrap around her waist.

"That's a great dress," I said, "ideal for camouflage. But aren't you worried about getting dirty?"

Alicia squinted at me and slid the sunglasses down from her head. They were oval-shaped with a tinge of lavender in the lenses. "No, not really."

"Let's do this!" Joy urged in her best rally-the-troops voice. All the same, I could see the swimsuit straps poking out from under her tank top, which meant Slip 'N Slide was still somewhere on her mind.

"I don't see why it's such a big deal," Alicia said. "They're just ordinary stairs." She started out walking ahead of us, but soon Joy and I were bounding past her, gleeful in our blatant disregard for family rules.

On this day we made no pretense of blackberry-picking. We had come for one reason only: to expand the map, to broaden our horizons in the most literal sense of the phrase. After fifty-six steps, weedy and steep and uneven as they were, we arrived on the landing, flushed and tousled, the curls around our temples matted to our cheeks. Alicia completed the ascent calmly, leaned against the railing, and searched her little purse for gloss. "Like I said, every morning I stand here and wait for my ride. I don't know what you think is going to happen."

But to see it—to see our very own neighborhood from such great height—Joy's street and my street tiny lines in the distance, like the view from airplanes or swooping movie cameras! What a dollhouse world it was! Small after all—the tree-tops, the chimneys, the ferry dock and far-off islands. Joy and I grinned at each other, laced hands, and spun in circles, singing, "It's a small world after all, it's a small world after all . . ."

Alicia, weary of us already, gestured toward a gravel driveway hardly visible between the neat rows of manicured homes. "In case you're interested, the Buddhist center is over there."

Joy and I stopped mid-chorus to consider Alicia's words. We had done plenty of investigating within a parent-approved radius, but we were rogue now, officially off the grid, and we needed to see it through.

"OK. It's a place of business, right?" I reasoned aloud. "People must go down there for consultations or classes or other kinds of Buddhist things. What do Buddhists do?"

"They practice nonattachment," Joy said with confidence. "Some of my mom's best friends are Buddhists. That's how I know."

"But do you have to practice nonattachment in a group setting?"

"No. I think Buddhists are pretty flexible."

"And they're nonviolent, right?" I asked so as to calm my nerves about the ultimate trespass into unfamiliar terrain.

"Definitely," Joy said.

"Then, let's do it. Let's pretend we're just walking down the driveway to find out a little more about Buddhism. There might even be pamphlets we can pick up to make us seem more legit." Joy and I headed off together, then turned back.

"Are you coming with us, Alicia?"

"I can be the lookout if you want." Even when she was just standing still, somehow Alicia seemed like she was posing.

"You can be the lookout if *you* want," I tell her, "but I want you to join us."

Alicia smiled wider and wider until she was showing her gums and even giggling a little, until she seemed almost like a regular girl. "Really?"

"Yes, really," I said, tugging her arm. "We'll make a gumshoe out of you yet."

The Buddhist meditation center was just a rickety white house with a few parking spots and a porch overgrown with black-eyed Susans. "Maybe it's abandoned," Alicia whispered.

"Maybe. Or it could be that they're just not attached to making the place look good. How are your haunted vibes, Joy?" I was intrigued by ghosts from a theoretical stance, but Joy had a better track record with actual paranormal encounters. To date, she had seen at least three unexplained figures floating in her home.

"I'd say we're at moderate to heavy haunting here. Let's go around back."

The blackberry bushes formed a barbed hedgerow from behind, slowly encroaching on the house itself. They had all but swallowed a chrome fender left out in the yard, and I could imagine them winding along the front steps and then climbing higher toward the derelict roof. But along the right side of the house, we moved freely, skirting the window wells and the occasional, errant shingle half-hidden in the grass.

"I want to look inside," Alicia said. Her voice was soft still, but her tone was earnest.

"Here," I said. "Put your foot in my hands, and I'll give you a boost."

Joy leapt toward me like the gazelle she was. "Me, too!"

"So, what do you see?" I asked Alicia as she propped her chin on the window ledge and peered inside.

"It's dark, but it looks like there are candles."

"Are they lit?"

"I think so, but they could be electric. I think they're the kind you see at Christmas."

"My turn!" Joy insisted.

She was able to hoist herself higher and balance on her hands. "I see pillows arranged in a circle on the floor."

"Sleeping pillows?"

"No, more like cushions—the square kind for sitting on."

Together, Alicia and Joy cupped my feet and tried their best to lift me to the ledge. We avoided the subject of my larger bones, my greater weight, and for this, I was grateful. I pressed my belly against the bricks and did my best to balance there, pressing my face against the glass so hard I made a sweat-smudge. I took note of the candles—electric or battery-powered, I wasn't sure which—and the cushions studded with animal shapes and tiny mirrors. Then, a woman in a loose head scarf appeared, materializing in the stark light of the room, and made a beeline for the curtains. I gasped and, for the second time in two days, plummeted to the ground.

The woman was knocking on the window, and I was dirty again—my knuckles scraped and freckling with blood as I shouted "Run! Run!" We were frightened, sure, but excited too, sensing what a disappointment it would have been if nothing had happened. We pumped our legs through the weeds and wildflowers, over the gravel that hurt our feet a little, especially mine in my thin-soled, knockoff shoes. We were so busy looking back over our shoulders that we didn't expect to collide with someone standing at the top of the driveway, beating on the rusted mailbox and talking to himself in a low chant-rhyme.

I screamed as my body made contact with his. He flailed his arms but didn't retreat. When I took a second look, I realized he was just a boy, not much older than I, his hair a nest of messy curls, his jeans black and dusty and his shirt black and dusty, too.

I stopped—literally, there in my own dusty tracks—and asked him, "Hey, are you a Buddhist?"

He looked away and resumed beating the mailbox—more like a drum this time, with a steady rhythm.

"Are *you*?"

"Julie, let's go!" Joy was breathless and calling from the top of The Stairs.

The boy shook his head, then said, "I'm a genius," without meeting my eyes.

When I turned again, I saw Alicia, her shoulders slumped, her composure lost. She pleaded with me tearfully, "Julie, please, just go with Joy."

I looked from her to the boy and back again. He had raised the red flag on the mailbox and begun to wander off down the unfamiliar street. He seemed to be reciting a long string of numbers then, but there were curse words too, mixed in.

"What is it? What's wrong? I think he's harmless," I said.

"Please, Julie, just go with Joy!"

The boy was moving faster then, half-walking, half-skipping, further away from The Stairs. I noticed for the first time that his feet were bare.

"Lawrence!" Alicia called after him. "Lawrence, come back here!"

"You know him?" I asked, astonished. "You know that boy?"

She was running by then, waving her hands like a coach calling for Time Out. "Larry! Larry!"

"Is he someone from the meditation center?" I called after her.

"Shut up about the center, will you?" she sobbed. All the velvet in her voice was gone, replaced by hard, guttural sounds. She couldn't even muster a polycotton blend. "Don't you get it?" Alicia was halfway up the street before she turned around. "He's my brother!"

My diary was going to get an earful about the day's events, but Joy made me promise not to bring up Lawrence around Alicia. "Everyone has something they'd rather not talk about," she said, seeming very mature all of a sudden.

"Did you know she had a brother?"

"Sort of," Joy said. "I knew she wasn't an only child, but I think her parents try to pretend she is." She waved as we parted ways at the corner of Vashon View Street, the cul-de-sac where Joy lived with her mom and dad and little brother Raphael. "I'm sure if Alicia ever wants to talk about it, she will."

The next day Alicia didn't call, but it was just as well because my mother and grandmother were taking me back-to-school shopping at Sears. "She's growing like a weed," my mother sighed. "All her pants from last spring are already past the high-water mark—and those broad shoulders. Don't even get me started!"

"Julie, dear," said Grandma June, turning around in the front seat and smiling at me. "I hear you have a new friend—the Fischer girl." She had a knack for knowing things like that, even though she mostly sat in her house all day reading books and working crossword puzzles. I often wondered if my grandmother, too, led a secret life as a sleuth.

"Oh, Alicia," I answered cautiously. "She's Joy Meyerowitz's friend from dance, but she's definitely becoming my friend, too, I think."

"Fischer? Why is that name familiar?" my mother asked.

"They bought the huge house at the top of 39th Avenue, western side, the one that was on the market forever."

"The brown one?" my mother repeats. "That *monstrosity* you can see all the way from Barton?"

"It's really pretty inside," I volunteered. "The Fischers have amazing taste!" I moistened my lips to pass on what I'd learned. "They're minimalists, and they collect art, especially Asian art because European art is so commercial these days."

My mother eyed me in the rearview, her whole face set on frown. "Since when have you been spending time *inside* the house of people I've never met?"

"Well, she is a friend of Joy's, and their families know each other, so I figured it was OK when Mrs. Fischer invited us in for cookies and lemonade. That was just two days ago," I said, my fingers forming a nervous knot. "If she had poisoned anything, I'm sure I'd be dead by now."

"Don't be smart!" my mother snapped.

"I wasn't. I'm just saying that Mrs. Fischer is nice, and—she even gives Alicia a shopping allowance so she can buy her own clothes."

I watched my mother and grandmother exchange silent glances in the front seat.

"Well, if you think you're going to get an allowance to buy your own clothes, you've got another thing coming. I won't have my daughter running around looking like a ragamuffin. It's hard enough to keep you in anything clean."

I watched my mother's nostrils flare in the mirror, and my grandmother, our perennial peacekeeper, turned to me again and tried a different approach. "You know, Julie, sometimes you hear about something that sounds good from a distance, and you think you want it for yourself. My Linda," referring now to my father's younger sister, "always wanted to pick out her own clothes, but she didn't know where to look for the best deals or how to find the fabrics that would be the most durable. That's why it's good to have a mother who takes care of you and doesn't leave you to your own devices."

I wanted to protest that Alicia Fischer was the best-dressed girl in any third grade anywhere and that her mother was understated and classy in a way my mother, with her robin's-egg eye shadow and gold lamé accessories, would never be. I wanted to reveal to them that Mrs. Fischer was the only reason I came home wearing an eyelet blouse that was cleaner at the end of the day than when I went out to play. *She was even better at laundry than my mom.* But instead, I made my voice small and agreeable, the way I tried to make my body small and agreeable, and curled my lips in a churchy smile.

"Oh, I know," I said. "I was just telling you what the Fischers do. I wasn't asking to buy my own clothes."

Alicia and I resumed playing together soon afterwards, pretending that she didn't have a secret brother. She liked sleuthing and started dog-walking with Joy and me to gain experience spying on the neighbors. I learned to take my shoes off in her parents' foyer—first, I had to learn what a foyer was—and to wash my hands twice with antibacterial soap before I handled anything, food or otherwise, in her house. Alicia, it did not escape my noticing, only had to wash once.

The weekend after Halloween, Alicia called to invite me over for a pumpkin party. I could hear the excitement percolating in her throat, but still I had to ask, "Doesn't a pumpkin party usually happen in October?"

"Oh, that's a pumpkin-*carving* party," she said. "This is something else."

"OK," I said. "Should I call Joy?"

"She's sick," Alicia replied. "Her mom won't let her come because she's running a fever."

I agreed to head over to the Fischer house just as soon as I finished my chores, and then Alicia added, cryptic as ever, "Bring your money, too. My mom might take us shopping after."

In the past year, I had earned close to thirty dollars from my cut of the dog-walking business alone. If you counted the money my grandmother paid me to pull weeds in her garden and the remunerations for watering a few neighbors' lawns while they were on vacation, the grand total in my tin was forty-five dollars and some change. This was pure profit, since I had already tithed my ten percent at church.

I worked hard for this money, and my father promised there was no satisfaction like money you had earned "by the sweat of your brow." He worked in an office with air-conditioning, so I wasn't sure how much he actually sweated to earn his money. But I had sweated for every penny in my tin and had the sunburns and stinky clothes to prove it. Strangely, though, I was sweating in a different way now—the guilty sweat of a bandit reaching for a cash box. As I folded the rumpled bills and stuffed the thick wad into my pocket, my heart began a drum solo in my ears.

I forgot about the money for a little while as Alicia and I carried softly rotting pumpkins to the bottom of the road. At our house, there was one pumpkin every year. I picked it from the box outside the supermarket, and my father and I carved it together at the kitchen table with a steak knife. The eyes were either upside down or right side up triangles, the nose could be a circle or a square, and the mouth had just a big gash for a smile. If he was feeling especially artsy, my father might cut a few small teeth into the grin. Then, we scooped out the seeds and set a votive candle in the belly that glowed all month long as we ate our meals and played after-dinner games at the table.

The Fischers, not surprisingly, took pumpkin carving to another level. They bought pumpkins of all sizes, including the white ghost pumpkins I had long admired. On some of them, they had painted a range of emotions, indicating fright or delight or surprise; others they carved using special pumpkin stencils to represent a lion with a full mane or a panther with wild, cunning eyes.

"Why are we putting these in the middle of the street?" I asked.

"Because," Alicia smiled, "we're going to drive over them."

"We are?"

"It's a tradition," she said. "Now that we live on such a big hill, the splat is going to be so much better."

As we piled the pumpkins near the intersection of 39th and Trenton Avenues, I notice that one—large, white, and lopsided—was more elaborately decorated than all the others. The pumpkin was really just the canvas for an extravagant scene: a child turning cartwheels, another flying a kite. There were even birds, their wings spread in flight, disappearing into the background.

"Is this from a stencil?" I asked.

Alicia, with a quick glance: "No. I don't think they even make stencils that advanced."

"Who made it then? Was it you? Was it your mother?"

She shook her head, tugging the gray knit cap over her ears. "It was Lawrence. He's kind of visionary like that."

"Does he go to school?" I looked away from her as I spoke, thinking it would make me seem casual, noninvasive. All around us the dead leaves swirled.

"No. I mean, he *has,* in the past, but it never turns out well. Mostly, tutors just come to the house. It's easier that way. He's already doing fourth-dimensional geometry."

"Are you girls ready?" A man at the top of the hill waved his gloves in the air.

"That's my dad," Alicia said. "I'll race you," and then she leapt forward with a sudden jolt of power.

The garage was open at the Fischer house, gaping like a mouth midsentence. Mrs. Fischer wore a long sweater cinched at her hips with a fabric belt. She said she'd watch us, but she wasn't going to ride.

"Dad, this is Julie," Alicia said.

Mr. Fischer was a petite (could we say this about men?), elegant man who wore a sport coat even on Saturday. Clean-shaven with a cleft in his chin and small, darting eyes that never stopped moving, Mr. Fischer also had tapered fingers, sleek and hairless like those of the man who played the grand piano in Rainier Square. They were beautiful (could we say this about men?), but soon he slipped his hands into a pair of brown, leather gloves.

"Good, very good," Mr. Fischer nodded by way of greeting. "Let's proceed to the car."

"Which car?"

"The Mercedes," he directed.

"I love that it's green," I whispered to Alicia.

"Oh, that wasn't our choice. It used to belong to my grandma." We slid in through separate doors and met in the middle. "She lives in Tampa, Florida, where anything goes."

Up and down the hill we went, hitting the pumpkins hard every time, then backing over them in bumpy repetition.

"Did you know there's a band called Smashing Pumpkins?" Alicia beamed.

"We should get a tape of their music to play while we do this!"

Mr. Fischer was silent, mechanical in his task. I wondered what was in it for him, what pleasure he found in the sharp acceleration and the fitful reverse. *Wasn't this his family ritual after all?* When nothing remained but a heap of mangled pulp, he made a smooth U-turn and guided the green Mercedes expertly back to the garage.

"Ask your mother to get a car wash while she's out," he instructed Alicia.

"Do we clean it up—the pumpkin mess, I mean?" I scanned the immaculate walls for some sign of a shovel.

"That's what city workers are for. Let them take care of it." The door slammed shut and, a moment later, Mrs. Fischer appeared again, this time in her tam and mittens.

"Dad requested a car wash," Alicia told her mother.

"Fine. I'm going to drop you girls at Westwood Village. I need to make a trip to the bakery and the deli, too. It should take at least an hour. Where would you like me to meet you?"

"L. A. Connection." Alicia spoke with clarity and precision, the way everyone in her family did—well, everyone except the one I couldn't name. There seemed no room for stumbling in their world, but perhaps no room for celebrating either. Every act was conducted with the same high level of scrutiny and decorum. "Have you ever been to L. A. Connection?"

I shook my head. "I've never even heard of it."

Washington Mutual, my parents' bank, was about the only reason we even went to Westwood Village anymore, now that the Winchell's Donut House had closed. My mother distrusted stores that weren't well-established, and she was quick to point out that most of the shops and restaurants there went bankrupt and were replaced within a year.

But Alicia led me to L. A. Connection as if in pursuit of the Grail. "What makes these clothes so special?" I prodded.

"I'm not going to lie to you," she said. "They're not of the same quality as Nordstrom's or The Bon or any of the dress boutiques downtown." I had never been to a dress boutique, and when I thought about it, I had only been to Nordstrom's once to use the bathroom. "But if you want to finesse your wardrobe, everything in this store is from California." Alicia said California the way our pastor said *Amen* after a reading from the Gospel. She was certain; it was so.

I thought of the money in my pocket as Alicia glided between the racks, accumulating items.

"Do you need some help?" a teenage girl with hoop earrings called from across the room.

"We're fine, thank you," Alicia replied with a jaunty lift of her arm. "It's all the latest trends," she said, almost bragging, as if this store were her very own brainchild. "If I wanted a makeover, this is the first place I'd come."

I looked down at my brown, corduroy pants, my pale blue turtleneck, and matching brown, corduroy vest. I felt my stomach churn as I said it aloud: "I look like Oliver Twist." Alicia continued her busy wheedling through the hangers. "I do, don't I? I look like Oliver Twist."

"Well, at least you're not wearing a corduroy cap," she said. "And I think penny loafers can be OK if you take out the pennies." Sadly, the pennies were my favorite part.

Under the ominous fluorescence of the fitting-room lights, I tried on eleven pairs of leggings. They all had a cuff of lace around the bottom, which Alicia explained was in vogue. I liked the leggings, how light they felt on my body compared to the heavy pants. Whenever I got caught in the rain in my corduroys, I felt like I was going to drown.

"Some of your clothes are sacky," Alicia observed. She spoke like a doctor making a diagnosis. "You have a solid build, but you're smooth everywhere. You don't need all this extra room in your pants and shirts. The idea is to keep it simple, keep it sleek."

I tried on some long sweaters, too, cable-knit with V-necks and asymmetrical shoulders. I even tried a tunic that cinched at the side with chunky buttons that resembled jewels.

"One more thing," Alicia said, dropping something over the half-sized door.

"What is this?" I felt the heft in my hands. "A sweatshirt?"

"Not just any sweatshirt. It's an *L. A. Raiders* sweatshirt."

"But this is bulky," I said, studying the large icon of a man's grizzled face. He wore a black patch over one eye, and two swords seemed to crisscross behind his head. "Is a raider a pirate?" I asked. "Is he a thief—a bounty hunter?"

"It's a football team," Alicia replied, and I noted the subtle annoyance in her tone. "If you wear this sweatshirt, you are sending a message."

I pulled it over my head and instantly felt the soft fleece stick to my sweaty skin. "What message?"

"That people better take you seriously—or else."

I spent all but my last four dollars at L. A. Connection. The leggings were on sale, so I got two pairs—black and purple. The tunic seemed too flashy, so I opted for a green sweater that stretched almost to my knees, and at Alicia's insistence, I bought the Raiders sweatshirt, too.

"When you wear that," she whispered, "you won't even need a coat."

"If there's a problem with any of the merchandise," the clerk said, "you have thirty days to return it for in-store credit or exchange. We don't, can't, and won't offer returns." She studied my face to make sure I understood.

Nodding, I foisted my fistful of cash into her outstretched hand, then tucked the skimpy receipt into my pocket. I felt lighter already. When Mrs. Fischer arrived, she cooed over my purchases and suggested I would look especially striking in green. "I think green is your power color," she said. Then, we waited while she bought a cappuccino at the coffee stand. "Would you girls like anything?"

"A cremosa, please," Alicia said, but since all these words were foreign to me, I smiled and politely declined.

I had been so busy dreaming of a way to move effortlessly through my days like Alicia Fischer and her mother that I failed to consider how my own mother would react when she saw my new clothes. *I've done nothing wrong,* I kept reassuring myself as the realization began to dawn. I wasn't a raider; I had earned the money and spent it as I saw fit. Surely, this was reasonable. Surely, my mother would understand. But when I rang the bell on my own doorstep, I stashed the L. A. Connection bag behind a flowerpot. I decided at the last possible second that it was safer to proceed with empty hands.

About an hour later, when my father returned from hauling yard waste to the dump (we always seemed to have too much for the regular bins), I heard his cheerful voice in the hall. "Someone left this bag on our porch," he said. "Looks like clothes. Maybe something for your charity drive, Linda?"

"No!" I shouted. My own voice startled me it was so loud. "That's mine!" But before I could swipe the bag from his hand, my mother went for the interception.

"What in the world—" The clothes scattered on our living room carpet: purple, black, green, a collage of colors, and then the L. A. Raiders sweatshirt, which my mother seemed to find particularly incendiary.

"Bill? Do you see this? I need a witness here."

"I didn't know you were interested in football," he said, turning to me with a light in his watery blue eyes.

"This is what *gangsters* wear!" my mother shrieked after a moment's contemplation. "Where's your big cross necklace and your red bandana and your *gun?*"

My dad looked at me, bewildered. I looked down at the shiny pennies in my shoes.

"Who gave you permission—"

"It's *my* money," I said suddenly. "I earned it, and I can spend it as I see fit." Even though I had rehearsed the words in my head before, they wobbled out of my mouth like unreliable, wind-up toys.

"You think that's how it works around here? You're lucky I don't charge you rent for all the trouble you cause me! Now where is this store—*La Connection*—"

"It's *L. A.* Connection," I corrected. "All the clothes come from California."

"Give me the receipt!" my mother demanded. "I want to see just how much money you've wasted so you can what—dress like a hooligan? Get some boy who wears his pants around his knees and listens to rap music to take you for a ride in a stolen car?"

I didn't know anyone who was old enough to drive, but I could see this was beside the point.

"Linda, why don't we calm down a little?" my father proposed.

"Well, I'll tell you why *we* don't calm down a little, Bill. Two of us would have to be outraged for *we* to calm down, but there you go, being the permissive parent, letting Julie think she can always get her way because she has Papa Pushover in her corner."

"I don't think that," I said, trying to protect him. "We can go back to the store. I can find something else."

"Oh, you think you're getting something else? You'll be lucky if you ever get anything ever again!"

"Linda!"

"But it's just that—they don't take returns," I murmured. "I can only exchange the clothes for in-store credit."

My mother had never met a return policy she couldn't quibble with, but a *no*-return policy was absolutely unthinkable. "Get in the car! Get your coat, and get in the car!"

"Linda, I think it's good to have a little dialogue—" My father, looking helpless in an ill-fitting polo shirt and khaki slacks, tried to block her way.

"I'll deal with you later," my mother said, like he was secretly her son and not her husband. "Julie, you are going to give me that receipt, and we are going to get your money back. Then, I will take a twenty-percent surcharge for the hell you've put me through."

It was dusk when we pulled into the parking lot at Westwood Village. The sky crowded with inky clouds, and the last light slipped between them like a message under a door.

"Who put you up to this? Was it that Alicia Fischer? You know I haven't liked her from the start."

"No," I said, the tears coasting down my cheeks. "It was my idea."

"You didn't walk here by yourselves, did you? Because you know you're not allowed to go anywhere outside the neighborhood without a chaperone."

"I know. Mrs. Fischer drove us."

"And she stayed with you the whole time?"

"Yes." If I kept my voice flat, and my head down, a truth and a lie sounded like synonyms.

"All right. Let's go."

"Oh, I thought *you* were going to do it," I mumbled. "I thought you were going in to get the money back."

"Clean up your mess? Are you kidding? *You're* going to explain your mistake, and I'll be standing by to make sure your apology is accepted—and *refunded*."

My mother should have been wearing the Raiders shirt, I mused, but then again, she didn't really need it. I found her far more intimidating than any depiction of the team's mascot, really *any* team's mascot, and given how often customer service was called just as she arrived at a store, I doubted I was alone in this feeling.

We stepped out from the car into the unseasonable cold, our over-sized parkas crinkling in unison. "I heard from Shelly White that the Fischers have a son—a savant of some kind? Apparently, he's such a piece of work he can't even leave the house. They never take him anywhere."

My mother squatted down and checked her lipstick in the side mirror before we set off toward the store. When I didn't say anything, she pressed me: "*Well?* You've been to their house. You should know. Does Alicia have some kind of circus freak for a brother?"

"No," I said, thinking of my friend, her mother and father, how they all fit together like a three-piece suit, impeccably tailored. The Fischers made sense that way, and that's how I wanted to keep them, especially when everything else seemed about as mind-boggling as the concept of fourth-dimensional geometry.

With my voice flat, my head down, and my hands shoved deep in my pockets, I told my mother, "No, Alicia is an only child."

Mrs. Arlington

[Or a Study of Apocalypse as an After-School Special]

The thing you have to understand about Mrs. Arlington is that she wasn't *warm,* not like Mrs. Saunders, who was the warmest mother of them all. She wasn't gentle-pretty like Mrs. Newport, and she wasn't austere-pretty like Mrs. Fischer either. She was efficient and accomplished in her motherly role—after all, she had a lot of practice—but I think the adjectives that best described her were *practical* and *matter-of-fact.* It is also possible, though not confirmed, that she was lacking in imagination.

The Arlingtons bought the house where my parents used to live during the early years of their marriage. The house sits on a small bluff about a quarter-mile from where we live now, though it is smaller than our house and lacking a view of the water. Kristin is the oldest of the five Arlington children, and she explains to me in her practical, matter-of-fact way that even before she was born, there were others: "Two siblings. We don't know if they were boys or girls. My mother miscarried."

"What exactly does that mean?" I ask. We are straddling the fence overlooking her yard, shelling peanuts and feeding them to squirrels.

"It means she was with child, and then God decided to stop the pregnancy."

"So, the baby just vanished and her stomach got flat again over-night?"

"She hemorrhaged," Kristin replies, and when I look confused, she sighs like I am the stupidest person on earth, "—*started bleeding and bled the whole baby out.*"

This strikes me as quite disgusting, but at least with Kristin I am always learning new words.

Kristin is also the first friend I have ever had who comes from what can be properly called "a big family." Not only that, but her family operates by their own set of—some might say *rigid,* or *unimaginative*—rules. Kristin's father is a commercial airline pilot whose name tag says "Skip," but it turns out that's only a nickname. His real name is Kermit, like Kermit the Frog, but when I ask if he was named after the Muppet, she folds her arms and becomes im-possibly cross.

"It's a *family* name," she says. "It's been in our family for *years.* Kermit the Frog was probably named after *him.*"

"Oh," I say, "sorry."

But because Kermit's name starts with "K," all the daughters' names must start with "K," too. So far there is just *Kristin* and her lit-tle sister, *Karen.* "My parents are always trying to bring glory to God by having more children," she explains. "There could be a *Kayla* or a *Kara* in our family soon."

Because Mrs. Arlington's other name is Marilyn—though she is nothing at all like the movie star with the full white skirt and the red pouty lips whose image proliferates on lunch boxes and potholders and tins of saltwater taffy at beachside stores—all the sons' names must start with the same letter. They have *Mark,* who is just two years younger than Kristin, and *Michael,* who looks different around the eyes, and a brand-new baby, *Matthew,* who has just appeared in the single year I have known Kristin.

"Can you tell me more about Michael?" I ask. "The angel or my brother?"

"Your brother."

"Well, he was named after the archangel Michael, of course, the way Matthew and Mark were named after the New Testament writers."

"The Old Testament is more interesting," I declare, tired of being the one without opinions. "I think they should have named your brother *Jonah*."

"That doesn't follow the M-rule," Kristin snaps back like a blond rubber band. "OK, so—*Malachi*."

"Naming him after the angel helps us remember how close we are to God and how close God is to us."

"Is there something—*wrong* with him?" I venture. This is the good thing about Kristin: she values factual information more than she appreciates tact.

"He has Down's syndrome, which means he has an extra chromosome. God makes some people special so we can all remember that we are at His mercy—that He is the one who decides."

Tonight at my house we are having breakfast for dinner, which means my father is in charge—French toast dipped in egg batter and sizzling bacon and orange juice from a frozen can. My mother sits at the table with her glue gun, arranging seashells around a circular mirror, preparing to make an all-season wreath for our wall.

"Kristin told me about Down's syndrome today. She says Michael was born with an extra chromosome because God wanted us to remember how vulnerable we are."

"Well, that's a crock if I ever heard one," my mother replies.

"They always were a little strange with their religion," chimes my father.

"Down's syndrome is most likely to occur when a woman is too old to be having children," my mother clarifies. She comes to where I am standing and holds the cylinder of orange concentrate under a steady stream of hot water. "Bill, do you know how old Marilyn Arlington is?"

"I'd guess mid-forties," he says.

"She is *forty-eight* years old. Trudy Bigelow told me. Michael was born when she was forty-five, and this new baby"—she purses her lips—"well, when is enough enough?"

"The Arlingtons believe in Heaven-ordained procreation," I say, parroting my friend. "Kristin told me all about it. Plus, they have a wall hanging with that Bible verse about *go forth and multiply.*"

"What about *all things in moderation?*" my father retorts.

Clearly, he doesn't understand the rules. "Dad," I say, "that's a secular cliché. The first one comes straight from the Bible."

I have to admit, the Arlingtons *are* a little strange about their religion. For one thing, the kids aren't allowed to write letters to Santa Claus or go on Easter egg hunts or dress up for Halloween. In fact, when my favorite holiday comes around, Kristin misses the costume party and can't even bob for apples from the old whiskey barrel in Joy's backyard. Her whole family hunkers down in their basement and gathers around the fireplace that doesn't work and sings praise songs. If you ring their doorbell for any reason on Halloween night—to trick-or-treat or share your candy or just to say hello—you know they're in there—you can see the dull light flickering through the lower windows—but no one will come upstairs to answer the door.

"It's the Devil's holiday," Kristin elucidates. She has joined my dog-walking business, so now we stroll around the neighborhood with a motley crew of good-natured mutts and slow-footed cocker spaniels.

"But it's so fun," I protest. "It's the one day a year when you get to be somebody else."

"If you're right with the Lord," she says, all pert nose and smug intonation, "you don't need to change who you are. You don't even want to."

I look down at my shoes as if they are the key to my soul. I'm afraid to say it, but I think Kristin already knows. *I want to.*

"Kristin Arlington says she has seen her guardian angel," I tell Grandma June and Great Aunt Ruth who is visiting from Canada. "Do you believe that's possible?"

"Of course, dear. Anything is possible—Ruthie, shall I bring you some more coffee?"

"Yes, and let's have some cookies, too." Aunt Ruth is the oldest, thinnest woman I have ever seen, but her appetite rivals my own. She sits up to the table in her frilly pink blouse and her little knit cap with the floppy side flower she has crocheted herself.

"But if *anything* is possible, then doesn't that mean there might not even *be* angels—that there might not even *be* a God?"

Then comes a silence so deep I think I hear the house sinking further into the earth.

Aunt Ruth looks at me like I have just denied her dessert for three days.

"God is the given," my grandmother says at last. "And God makes all things possible."

It's clear I'm going to have to try a different approach with these people. "Well, have either of you ever seen your guardian angel?"

Aunt Ruth helps herself to three large oatmeal cookies and munches thoughtfully before she replies. "When Mac died, I felt a presence. I knew we weren't alone in that hospital room. I knew God had sent someone to bring him home to Heaven."

"But did you *see* anything? Some feathers? A bright light even?"

"I think you're missing the point, dear," my grandmother intercedes. "It's not what you see that's important. It's what you know in your heart is true."

My heart cannot be plumbed, let alone parsed into language. My heart is a pasture grown wild with vines, trampled by beasts, and newly overcome with clouds. But inside my mind, which I can picture like a long hallway that leads to a messy dressing room, I set about the task of sorting my thoughts into piles—what I've been told versus what I believe, what I doubt versus what I know for sure.

If I know it, I decide, *I'll drape it over my arm. If I doubt it, or if I can't be sure, I'll hang it back up on the rack.*

Everything I know from school returns to the rack because it is based on someone else's knowledge, someone else's promise that 8 times 8 means 64; that King Ferdinand and Queen Isabella of Spain sent Italian Columbus to the New World; that water really boils at 212 degrees F. Even *Fahrenheit* is something I take for granted, more of a hanger than a thought itself—something to hang an idea of temperature on. Before long, I am running out of hangers. I discover that most of what I think I know I haven't discovered for myself, least of all where God and angels and matters of salvation are concerned. Words have the effect of markers in a book, but even words aren't the real contents of the pages.

"Are you having a crisis of faith?" Kristin asks me, a look of concern on her typically stern, preadolescent face. She has just returned from ballet practice, her first year dancing *en pointe.* Even this is just a concept, I sigh. Someone decided to stuff cotton wool into flat-toed ballet slippers and call them pointe shoes. Someone decided girls should be twelve years old before they can wear them, but Kristin is only eleven and has been granted special permission by her teacher. For every rule, I see, there is also an exception, which makes nothing seem very *hard-and-fast,* nothing unalterably *so.*

"I don't know. That's just it. Suddenly, it's like I don't know anything anymore—not for sure—nothing that I can't poke holes through."

Kristin's room is yellow as a canary or as the high-hatted man who cares for Curious George. She used to share her room with Mark, and yellow is the agreed-upon, gender-neutral color. (Why isn't it pink or green? Why do we even *need* gender-neutral colors?) At one end of her bed is a painting of angels, each with a translucent robe and a tiny harp, serenading some shepherds in a field. At the other end is a framed photograph of pointe shoes, a whole row of them, dyed every vibrant color of the rainbow.

"First of all, if you're trying to poke holes through things, then you're not thinking like a good disciple of Christ. You're thinking like a person of this world."

"But I *am* a person of this world," I protest.

Kristin sighs and shakes her long shock of yellow hair. "Only in the technical sense—and only for a little while." As she unwraps the tape from her toes, I wince at the blood thickly crusted over her nails.

"Doesn't that hurt?"

"Of course—but it's worth it. Dancing is like the body's own way of praying, of giving thanks to God without words."

I have been dancing a long time, and it has never felt like an expression of praise to me. Of course I am a poor dancer, and my teacher doesn't think pointe shoes are in my future. So maybe the truth is different for everyone, inherently conditional. Maybe Kristin's body is praying while she pirouettes with perfect grace while my body is simply longing for a playground—or a pizza.

"Why don't you come to church with us?" Kristin offers. "The van seats eight, but we only have seven, and there are services almost every night of the week."

In my sailor dress and my scuffed patent leather shoes, I wait with Kristin on the sidewalk while Mrs. Arlington backs her Aerostar up the long, steep drive. "My father had to fly today," Kristin says, "but he always tells us he's closer to God that way and doesn't mind."

"What does your bumper sticker mean?" I inquire.

"Well, you know, if we were driving when the Rapture came, we'd all float up to Heaven and our car would probably crash."

"Oh," mulling it over. "So, what's the Rapture?"

Mrs. Arlington has just climbed out of the driver's seat as I say it. I think how she has the body of an umpire, lumpy and soft, how she should be out on the field calling plays and blowing whistles whenever a team wants to take a Time Out. Today she looks strangely like a human potato in her drab brown dress and flat penny loafers, but a polo shirt and catcher's mask would suit her well.

"Julie, why don't you sit up front with me? Kristin, you sit in back and help with the babies."

It is a long drive to the Casey Treat Christian Faith Center, and Mrs. Arlington notices right away that I didn't bring a Bible. "Check the glove box," she instructs. "There should be extras in there."

"It's not that I don't *have* a Bible," I say, feeling suddenly embarrassed. "It's only that they print what we need to read from it on our programs at church."

"So, you *are* familiar with church?" she clarifies, her eyes transfixed on the road and her jawline tight, her cheeks hardly moving as she speaks.

"Sure. I've been going to church my whole life."

"Do you know what kind of church it is?"

"Lutheran," I say proudly. "I come from a long line of Swedish Lutherans on my father's side. And my father helped convert my mother before they got married."

"What was she?"

This question is one I haven't thought of before. "Oh," I murmur, "I'm not sure. Nothing, I guess." *Was that possible?* "Her family doesn't go to church."

"The reason I ask," Mrs. Arlington begins in her cool, even tone, "is that you were asking Kristin back at the house about the Rapture. Does your church not discuss the Apocalypse?"

"I'm an acolyte," I say. "Are they related?"

"Not quite," she replies. "What have you learned about the end of the world?"

I search the ransacked dressing room of my mind for answers but find nothing. Even the mirror is foggy now, like someone has been breathing too hard.

"I've heard of it," I tell Mrs. Arlington. "My father always says 'It's not the end of the world' when I spill something, though my mother usually acts like it is. I guess I thought that was just an expression—" My voice trails off, and I resist the temptation to gulp.

"No, Julie, the end of the world couldn't be more real, and our life here on earth *hinges* on our preparation for life in Heaven. Christ is going to come like a thief in the night, and we have to be ready—whether we go to him first in death, or whether He comes to us."

"So, you're saying we might not have to die?" What an enormous relief to imagine! Since death is what frightens me most, I am anxious to endorse any prospect that suggests I may never have to face it.

"If the Rapture comes in your lifetime, and you are a true believer, Christ will lift you up to Heaven and spare you the Seven Years of Tribulation."

"That's when things get really bad," Mark interjects, a little candle-flame of a boy flickering in the image of his sister. "It'll be like watching a horror movie, but you'll get to watch it sitting on a cloud in Heaven."

"*Provided* you have a sure and proper faith," adds Mrs. Arlington, in that very practical, very matter-of-fact way.

The Arlingtons' church is more like a sports arena with bench seats than a regular sanctuary with pews. The ushers carry walkie-talkies, and the minister and all his assistants wear microphones clipped to their ties. Despite its high ceilings and extravagant organ and monumental wooden cross, the Casey Treat Christian Faith Center is ugly—so ugly I would call it "butt ugly," except Kristin insists "butt" is a bad word.

"No part of the body is ugly," she has stated on several occasions. "It's only ugly minds that make people think that way."

A brief glimpse of my inner dressing room—the floor desperate for a sweeping, the busted light bulb longing to be changed.

Casey Treat is a lithe, red-haired man with a greasy pompadour and a smile as suspicious as Ronald McDonald's. I dislike him instantly, though I can't be sure that his convictions are wrong—only his style of presentation.

"Are you ready?" he shouts, working the crowd into a frenzy. "Are you ready for the day when Jesus comes?"

A chorus of "Hallelujah!" and "Amen!" startles me from my semiconscious doodles. "Are you ready for Jesus to lift you up?"

Now everyone has leapt to their feet, and Kristin pulls me to standing, clapping her hands and swaying.

"But you know—not everyone is as blessed as we are. Not everyone is going to be lifted up by Jesus."

We sit down again, and Casey Treat strides the full length of the elevated aisle—like a runway model showing off his Christian armor.

"There are some among us who are going to be left behind." He pauses dramatically to wipe his brow. "Yes, even in this room, there are some who will be left behind—those with insufficient faith—those who have not loved Christ enough to let Him save them."

A low wail escapes the crowd's collective lips.

"And they are going to suffer *unspeakable things.*"

I look around, feel the acid churning in my stomach—the ache of digestion when there is nothing left to digest.

"It could be your child—or your parent. It could be your aunt or uncle or a distant cousin. It could be that woman you always see at the supermarket, the one who smiles and says hello and seems like such a kind soul—but she didn't know Jesus." He bows his head. "She didn't know Jesus, and where is she now?"

"In Hell!" someone shouts.

"That's right, Sister." He looks up, unbuttons his sport coat, brings his hands together as if in prayer. "That kindly woman you always see at the supermarket is *burning in Hell for all eternity.*"

I shudder—a full-body hiccup I can't control; Kristin glances at me and frowns.

"You have been *commissioned,*" Casey Treat resumes, walking backward toward the altar, arms outstretched. "You have been *commissioned* to *evangelize!* What does that mean? *To spread the Good News!*" He sends his arms Heavenward, and the congregation rises like the wave at a football game. "The blood of every man, woman, and child that you fail to save is on your hands. Do you want to stand before the altar of Christ with sinners' blood on your hands?"

The room is shaking its collective head. Boys with buzzed hair and black ties are snaking through the aisles, offering plates like flying saucers balanced on their palms. My father has given me a dollar for just this occasion, but when the plate passes by me, I clutch my purse close to my chest. Kristin arches her brows, gives me a nudge, but I have nothing I am willing to hand over.

"How come we never talk about the Apocalypse?" I demand to know. My mother is primping before her bedroom mirror while my father searches through the closet for his coat. I sit on the edge of their bed, swinging my legs and fretting.

"What is there to say?" she asks, indifferent to my concerns. "We won't be here when it happens."

"What if—*hypothetically*—we were?"

"Julie, you know that's not going to happen," my father replies, his voice steady as the operator repeating a number. "We're a Christian family, and we'll be with the Lord when the time comes. I don't see any reason to dwell on all this gloom and doom."

"But what about the people who aren't raptured?"—not daring to reveal my fear that I may be among them.

"Tough shit!" my mother retorts.

"*Linda!*"

"Well, it's true. Why should I feel sorry for them when they had their whole lives to get with the program?"

"But maybe they didn't!" I protest. "What about really little kids who can't talk yet, and animals, and people who don't speak English so they can't understand the Good News?"

"If this is what comes from playing with Kristin Arlington," my father says, folding a clean white handkerchief into his pocket, "then maybe you girls need to take a break from each other."

"Dad, there are going to be terrible monsters in the End Times! There are going to be plagues and famines and fires raging out of control—and Satan is coming to earth as a dragon with seven heads!" I am about to cry out that I have never seen my guardian angel, not even once (a sure sign of faithlessness), and that I will never dance on my tiptoes in pretty pointe shoes, and that because of this Rapture business, I may never even have a chance to fall in love. Instead, I bite my lip, plod across the room, and lean against the doorframe. He hugs me and lays a gentle hand on my head.

"Satan has no power over you as long as you put all your faith in the Lord. And that's where it is anyway, am I right?"

He looks down at me and wipes the tears from my cheeks. I nod my head, but inside I am quaking with the growing certainty of my unholy demise.

"Linda, she feels hot to me."

"She's fine, Bill."

"No, I think she's running a little temperature."

My mother approaches, annoyed with us both, and presses her cold hand to the front of my head. After a moment, her clenched lips loosen, and she takes me back to my bed.

While I am sick, which is a rare occurrence, I try to calculate the odds of the Rapture happening in my lifetime, the bitter irony of cheating death only to be left behind. *But maybe I won't be,* I reason, the thermometer lolling under my tongue. *If I believe the Rapture is a real possibility, then doesn't that constitute some measure of faith in God?*

My mother comes to take the thermometer out. She tells me to be still—an impossible imperative—then hands me two chewable, grape-flavored Tylenol and lays a cold compress over my eyes.

How much is enough faith? I wonder, thinking of a track star vaulting over a bar—how, sooner or later, even the best athletes fall back on the mat, chests heaving, legs wobbling beneath them, the bar at last having been raised too high.

As I fall to dreaming, swimming through the dark heat, I pass Kristin in her scuba gear, with her long-necked flashlight of perpetual preparation. She'll find her way to Heaven for sure, even if it is inexplicably underwater. When I wake, my mouth dry, sticky with saltine paste and the waste of a sun-filled afternoon, I attempt my prayer: *When is enough enough, God? How much certainty can you expect from me?*

"I don't understand how you're allowed to have a birthday party when you're not allowed to celebrate any of the other holidays."

Kristin wears a white dress with blue violets sewn into the fabric. Her new year has straightened her further, like an invisible zipper sliding up her spine. While I look on, she brushes her hair about a million times, admires herself in front of the vanity mirror. "Our birthdays are the anniversary of our creation. To celebrate a birthday brings glory to God."

"Where are your parents?" I ask, suddenly aware of the house in a silent thrall.

"It's Tuesday." She points to the clock like Vanna to the wheel. "Four thirty. *Hel-lo.* They're doing the Lord's work."

I sigh, unable to hide my disdain. When Mr. and Mrs. Arlington are doing the Lord's work, we have to stay in Kristin's room or go to the basement and watch Christian videos with Mark and the other kids. No making noise or playing games or using the main-floor bathroom—the one I like best—with the fluffy carpet and the colored toilet paper.

"They'll be done in time to make dinner, if that's what you're worried about," Kristin proclaims. "My dad is grilling tonight, and my mom is making a macaroni salad."

"So, what should we do in the meantime?" I ask, bored of her primping, her boasts of newly shaved legs and tireless *piqué* turns.

Now her hair falls around her shoulders, a golden spider web of static cling. "I have some scented stationery," Kristin says. "Do you want to write our wills?"

Later, in the kitchen, I offer to help Mrs. Arlington slice or peel, secretly hoping to be assigned a more dangerous task—pouring oil into a heated pan, for instance, or climbing up on a stool to root through the highest cupboards.

"I'll say one thing, Julie. Your parents have certainly instilled in you a fine set of manners."

It seems like a compliment, but I sense there is more behind it than simple praise, more behind her colorless eyes than what she is willing to say.

"Tell you what. Take a Ziploc bag and hold it out for me each time I say."

"Are these party favors?" I ask, watching as she drops a granola bar, a pack of dried fruit, and a York peppermint patty into each translucent sack.

When she doesn't reply, I rack my brain for an explanation. "Are they for Mr. Arlington when he flies? Kristin says layovers can be long, and he's bound to get hungry."

"No, dear," Mrs. Arlington says, and I am surprised by the softness of her tone, the replacement of my name with a term of tenderness.

"Well then, are they earthquake kits?" We are each required to keep a sealed bag filled with nonperishable items in our cubby at school. That way, when the Big One hits, we won't starve to death waiting to be rescued—provided we can make it through the rubble to our food.

Mrs. Arlington is concentrating on her task and seems at first not to hear me. Then, as we are loading the small sacks into a large box with rumpled cardboard flaps, she answers, "Rapture kits. These are for those not delivered in the Rapture."

I, Julie Marie Wade, being of sound mind and body (though having just recovered from a fever), do hereby bequeath all of my valuables to my friend, Kristin Suzanne Arlington, not to be shared with any of her many siblings, unless they outlive her, in which case Karen gets first dibs . . .

We drag the box down to the basement, stuff it under the stairs where my own parents store our Christmas tree and related decorations. Mrs. Arlington writes FOR THE RAPTURE in all caps with a black marker, then stops, then regards me a moment across her smocked shoulder, lips flat as a level on the picture frame of her face.

"Would you like one?" she asks, still holding the masking tape, hesitating before she makes the final seal.

"No, thanks," I decline, though I follow the box with my eyes as she pushes it further and further away, back between the Goodwill donations and the surplus hymnals. I make a memory of the spot, press it to the wall of my mind like an old-fashioned photographic plate, the kind that takes a long time to develop. On the little tab beneath the picture, I jot the words *Just in Case.*

Mrs. Bigelow

[Or a Study of Death as the Last Bouquet]

My family had known Trudy forever, long before she became Mrs. Bigelow. She and my aunt met in college—at Washington State—and Linda felt sorry for Trudy because she never pledged a single sorority. It was unclear if she had ever been invited to join.

"If you asked her now—and *don't*, by the way," Aunt Linda commands, slicing a melon on her mother's kitchen counter, "I'm sure she'd say she didn't want to be part of all that nonsense anyway. But who is she kidding? It's only natural."

"What is?"

"Girls want to be pretty, and they want to belong. Trudy never had an easy time with either one."

"So, you're saying she was—an ugly outcast?" I clarify.

"No, dear." Grandma June looks up from her crossword and frowns. "Be careful about putting words into other people's mouths."

When they graduated college in 1968, Linda and Trudy took a two-week trip to Hawaii. Linda, who was good at being pretty and at least pretending to belong, wore her platinum hair in a flip and let the kind men in the flowered necklaces carry her matching set of cream and caramel luggage. She wore bikinis on the beach, drank fruity spirits from coconuts, and never had to worry about being asked to dance. Someone in a sport coat would always offer his hand.

But Trudy hung back. She didn't smile at the men, preferred to pay her own tab, wouldn't drink a Singapore Sling unless she ordered it herself. Trudy wore awkward sarongs to cover her thighs and hid her eyes behind enormous Elton John glasses. "I always had the sense," my aunt confessed, "that Trudy was a little bit jealous of me."

Then, the girls returned to the mainland. Linda took a receptionist job and moved in with a roommate named Carol, who revealed her views on Women's Liberation. She didn't let men hold open doors for her. She smoked cigarettes, refused makeup, and stayed out some nights until dawn. My aunt always suspected Carol of using birth control.

"There's progressive, and then there's downright *promiscuous*. When women stopped setting the standards, they ruined men for the rest of us"—Linda's eternal lament.

Six months later, she was back living at home with her parents. Aunt Linda didn't find a new apartment or strike out on her own again until she was thirty. Even then, she didn't find a husband. But Trudy did. Trudy married Tim Bigelow and bought a house in Linda's parents' neighborhood—Fauntlee Hills. Trudy started spending time in married women's clubs, letting her left hand dangle to show off her diamond ring. Linda's brother and his wife, who eventually became my parents, also bought a house in Linda's parents' neighborhood. Trudy and Linda's brother's wife, who eventually became my mother, became neighbors, acquaintances, and ultimately friends.

And so it was that Trudy gradually exchanged her friendship with my unmarried aunt for her friendship with my married mother, who was also known in those parts and at that time as "the other Linda Wade." I'm not sure Aunt Linda ever forgave Trudy for replacing her with my mother. And I'm not sure my mother ever forgave Aunt Linda for being the original Linda Wade.

"So, this is the living room," Ellie announces, flapping her arms with an air of proud, if contrived, disdain. "The usual boring stuff—plates we aren't allowed to eat off of, curtains we have to keep closed so the sunlight won't fade the furniture. Blah, blah, blah. It's lame, but don't worry. We don't have to hang out in here."

Ellie doesn't mention the picture of her mother looming over the fireplace. I thought only rich English people with hunting dogs had their portraits made and displayed in their homes. But here is Trudy alone—in a teal pantsuit with low-heeled shoes, head cocked to the side, auburn hair heavily coiffed, against a blue-sky background and blinding, white walls.

"Is there a safe?" I ask, gesturing behind the glossy photograph and its embellished gold frame.

"What do you mean?"

"In the wall—a place where your parents hide their valuables?" *Has she never read Nancy Drew?* "You know, the kind you have to open with a combination lock?"

Ellie's nose wrinkles like an unopened rose. "I don't think we have one of those."

"Well, what about a surveillance camera then?" *Surely a picture like that must serve some more illicit purpose.* "Have you noticed if the eyes in the photograph ever move?"

"You're a silly girl," Ellie snickers. "That's just a picture of my mother on her fortieth birthday. It's not supernatural or anything. It's from Yuen Lui Studios. My mom says this way, when she's gone, we'll have something to remember her by."

Our next stop on the new-friend tour is the Bigelow family kitchen. Ellie says this is her favorite room in the whole house and that her mother lets her do most of the cooking.

"My mother doesn't let me make anything," I sigh. "I'm not allowed unsupervised in the kitchen at all, on account of the fact that I once blew up our microwave trying to make muffins."

"Did you use those metal muffin tins?" Ellie asks, confidently maneuvering around me in pursuit of milk, mixing bowls, and a box of chocolate pudding.

"How did you know?"

"Common error," she replies. "If you want to put metal in the microwave, you have to use the convection setting."

"How old are you again?" I ask, suddenly intimidated by Ellie's culinary maturity.

"Twelve—but my mother says I'm going on seventeen."

I wonder if this is because of her large breasts, which are always straining to break free from her shirt-fronts and flopping from side to side when she moves. "I think it's because my brother who's ten"—she looks at me, remembers my age, and whispers *sorry* out the side of her mouth—"is a complete dumb-ass. He can't do anything. He's a helpless loser who sits in his room and plays with his iguana all day."

"Is that some kind of code?" I inquire, thinking of Alicia's brother who humps his mattress loudly in the next room and of other brothers who take too long in the bathroom.

"No—he actually *has* an iguana, and he let it out of its cage, and now it's so big it's taken over our whole basement. Word of advice," Ellie says, pouring the brown powder into the bowl. "Don't ever have a brother—*or* an iguana."

She gauges my height and then looks from me to the highest cupboard. "Do me a favor and get down four parfait glasses, will you?"

"What are parfait glasses?"

Ellie snickers again. "They're tall and clear with ruffled edges. You put parfaits in them."

"I don't think I've ever had a parfait," I confess, feeling around on the top shelf to find what Ellie has commissioned.

"Well, you will. I'm going to layer this chocolate pudding with

Cool Whip, three layers deep, and in about half an hour, we'll have two parfaits apiece."

"What are we going to do in the meantime?"

"You'll see," she says, and after we cover the parfaits with Saran wrap and put them in the fridge, I follow Ellie down the twisty hallway to her room.

Ellie's bedroom is spacious and elegant, more the province of a grown woman than of a preteen girl. She has a magazine stand featuring titles like *Bon Appétit* and *Country Living*, a floral daybed with brass posts, and a cavernous closet that whorls back in the wall like a seashell. Ellie steps inside and returns carrying a long, mysterious box.

"How do you feel about witchcraft?" she asks.

I trace the bold, black letters with my fingers: **O-U-I-J-A**. "I feel all right about it," I say at last.

"Well, have you ever conducted a séance or contacted a dead relative?"

I shake my head, feeling like a novice again.

"What about fortune-telling? Palm-reading? Tea leaves? Anything?"

"Mostly, I just play outside," I say, dropping to the floor and following Ellie's movements with my eyes. She collects an assortment of colorful, half-burnt candles and a book of matches and comes to sit beside me, her legs spread wide like a triangle.

"If you could talk to anyone who has crossed over to the Other Side, who would it be?" she inquires, lighting the candles and arranging them in a star shape on the silver serving tray.

"My grandfather, I guess. He's the only person I really know of who has died, and he died before I was born."

"Good," Ellie says. "Well, not *good*, but at least now we have a focus. We're going to see if we can contact your dead grandfather and get some answers. Family secrets. Whatever you want to know." She claps her hands, and all the lights dim. "Not magic," Ellie explains. "It's the Clapper."

"Oh"—but my heart is pulsing loudly in my ears. "Right. The Clapper."

"Put your hands here," she instructs, placing them on a small piece of plastic with a magnifying lens inside. Ellie lays her warm, doughy hands on top of mine and guides the planchette slowly across the board. "We're going to ask a question, and when your grandfather is ready to respond, he'll spell the answer out, letter by letter."

I am about to ask whether my grandfather approved of the woman my father decided to marry—also known as my mother or "the other Linda Wade"—when a black shape bursts forth from the closet, pounces on my chest, and claws my forearms with long streaks that draw blood. I scream and roll back, convinced God has sent a hairy demon to punish me for dabbling in the occult.

"Aloysius!" Ellie shrieks, clapping her hands so all the lights come on at once. "Aloysius, what's the matter with you?"

I look over in time to see a scruffy terrier disappear behind the door.

"That's our Scottie dog," Ellie murmurs. "He's been acting really weird lately."

I am too stunned to speak, too stunned to express my irritation that Ellie has warned me about the basement iguana but neglected to mention her dog. All I can do is stare at my arms, which are white and red like candy canes, a set of deep stripes stretching from wrist to elbow.

"Here," she offers. "Let me get you a long-sleeve shirt. You can freshen up in the bathroom if you want."

I take the jersey from her outstretched hand, still gaping in pain and surprise. "Just make sure your parents don't see those marks," she says, kneeling on one leg to blow out the candles. "You could get my dog sent back to the pound." Her voice turns low and raspy again. "Back to the pound—*or worse.*"

That night at dinner, my father teases me about the jersey. "That's about six sizes too big for you, Smidge," he laughs. "Where'd you get it?"

"Oh, this is Ellie Bigelow's. We were having—kind of a costume party." I flush and gulp my milk, hoping no one will notice my scratched arms beneath the baggy sleeves.

"I didn't know you knew Ellie," my mother remarks, scooping the cooked spinach like dripping sea slime onto our plates.

"We just met today," I tell her casually. My mother doesn't like it if she thinks I'm keeping secrets.

"I wouldn't imagine you and Ellie have much in common. How did you meet?"

"Playing—at Pine Cone Island."

"I didn't think Ellie was interested in outdoor recreation." My father stirs his words into the conversation slowly, studying my mother for some cue as to how he should proceed.

"She is, but . . ." I spin my fork like a carousel pole, round and round without ever lifting the spinach to my mouth. "Later, we went to her house and made pudding. Well, technically, *parfaits*."

"Julie," my mother says in a serious tone that frees us all from eating for a while, "there are a few things we need to discuss about Ellie Bigelow—especially if you plan on seeing her again."

I shrug. "She's nice. I like her." Plus, I am still hoping we can confer with my grandfather about the yet-unspoken question that weighs heavy on my mind.

"Was anyone home at the Bigelow house when you were there?" my father inquires.

"I don't know. She has a key, though—and there's an iguana in the basement."

"Ellie is a latch-key kid," my mother proclaims, with the solemnity befitting a funeral. "Both of her parents work full-time, and she and Brian have basically raised themselves."

"But I thought you were friends with her parents. I thought you *liked* the Bigelows."

"We *are* friends," my father clarifies, "but that doesn't mean we approve of certain things about their lifestyle. We believe, for instance, that mothers should be around for their children, and we also believe grown men shouldn't cheat at board games."

"Bill, that's not relevant here," my mother interjects. "The point is, Julie, it's fine if you want to see Ellie Bigelow *occasionally,* but we'd prefer it if you only visited her when one of her parents is home. She can always come here—*with advanced notice*—but I like to know there's someone keeping an eye on you two."

Now my heart thuds hard at my feet. *They knew about the Ouija board. They may have even known about the deranged Scottie dog and the afternoon's aborted séance.* "But Ellie's twelve," I protest. "She knows how to take care of herself."

"I think Ellie knows how to bake a lot of brownies and sit around on her ass."

"*Linda*—language!" My father winces and pats my arm. I wince and remove it from the table.

"Well, it's true, Bill, and it's time someone addressed the *other* issue here." My mother lifts her fork again like a gavel. "Julie, let's face facts. Ellie Bigelow is a *fat* girl. I'm not saying she isn't also a *nice* girl, but she's not the kind of girl you want to spend too much time with."

"You spend a lot of time with Trudy Bigelow," I retort, "and she isn't very thin—or very pretty." I don't know why I am lashing out at Mrs. Bigelow. It isn't her fault that nobody wanted her in their sorority.

"Julie, when you're young and impressionable like you are, you can easily pick up bad habits from your friends." My father has removed the napkin covering his tie and holds it gingerly between his hands. "What if you started eating with Ellie Bigelow every day? What do you think would happen to your figure?"

I hold my breath the way I do underwater, but my mother will not let this conversation drown. "These are hard truths, but you have to face them, Julie. Ellie Bigelow isn't going to get anywhere socially, being the size that she is. We don't want you to miss out on opportunities to—be invited to parties or—go out on dates—all because people associate you with"—she takes a bite of her spinach and chews it thoughtfully—"a certain type of person."

"You think I might not get dates because Ellie Bigelow is fat?" I repeat.

"Julie," my father sighs, slicing into his spare rib now, anxious for the conversation to end, "don't put words in other people's mouths."

Ellie's father Tim is a friendly man who likes to mow his lawn. This is not a euphemism either. He has a stressful job somewhere downtown and finds working in the yard a pleasant way to unwind. He and my father have conferred about the relaxing quality of yard work many times over an idling power mower or the synchronized swish of their brooms. What's more: Mr. Bigelow actually enjoys gardening. He plants flowers and tends a small crop of apple trees that Ellie calls her "magic orchard." In our family, my mother is the master gardener, but Mrs. Bigelow can't be bothered with making things grow. She has a stressful job too, and she'd rather watch game shows while Ellie pumices her feet than spend hours kneeling in the soil beneath leaf-choked gutters fending off mosquito swarms.

"See? What did I tell you? My dad has a really green thumb." Ellie and I are picking tart green apples in the Magic Orchard like characters in a Lucy Maud Montgomery story. The orchard is surrounded by a crumbling stone wall and a tall fence that is something other than picket but not quite cyclone either. These are the only kinds of fences I know. Our mission: fill a large wicker basket with apples so Ellie can bake a pie.

"I'm going to make the dough from scratch and then weave a lattice over the top and sprinkle it with brown sugar," she boasts. "You can stay if you want to. For the main course, I'm doing macaroni and cheese."

"With tuna fish or hot dog bits?" I ask, salivating a little.

"Both, if you want. My secret is that I use an extra packet of cheese so the noodles are super creamy and neon orange."

Looking around, I change the subject on purpose, guilty for having come here knowing no one is home: "Did your dad really grow all these flowers himself?" There are flamboyant orange nasturtiums, azaleas red as racing stripes, purple rhododendrons dense enough to form a hedge—and these are just the plants I recognize. Plus, of course, the roses. Tim's roses. So many and so lush I think of a phrase I love from *The Secret Garden:* "curtains and fountains of roses!"

"Yeah. He thinks no one appreciates them, though. My brother won't do anything in the yard unless he gets to use a power tool, and my mom doesn't come out here much, even though my dad bought her those fancy lounge chairs." Ellie gestures toward the patio. "I'm not supposed to tell anyone, but my dad doesn't sleep here anymore."

"Is he a traveling salesman?" I ask, recalling the lonely years when my own father was.

"No." She shakes her brown, self-braided hair and sighs. "He has an apartment where my mother makes him stay. She says they're having troubles, and they've been having them for a long time. But he still comes by to water the flowers and put nectar in the hummingbird feeders."

I can't tell Ellie what I have heard my parents discussing at home. My mother says that Trudy told her once how she only married Tim because she thought she couldn't do any better.

"She didn't want to end up an old maid, and who could blame her? She didn't want to end up like your sister."

"Let's leave Linda out of this," my father said, and I could hear the grimace in his voice even from the top of the stairs.

"He bought her a diamond, and she said 'I do,' but only because there was no one else in line."

"Surely she's exaggerating." My father's voice was low and sad. "People don't make lifetime commitments if there isn't love involved."

"Oh, Bill, wake up!" my mother scolded. "It boggles my mind to think how naïve you really are."

Ellie offers me an apron as she begins to wash the apples. I decline and sink down to the kitchen floor instead, my back propped against the dark wood cabinets. "Any chance we could try that séance again?"

"Sure—after I get the pie in the oven. Do you want some Oreo cookies while we wait?"

I think about it, tempted but afraid. "No, that's OK. My mom says no snacks before dinner, or I'll ruin my appetite."

"You're such a good girl," Ellie laughs, reaching for the cookie jar with her one dry hand.

"What do you mean?" I'm not sure whether to be flattered or offended.

"Just that you always want to do the right thing, or at least not make anybody mad at you. Like if I got mad at you right now—I bet you'd eat a cookie just to keep the peace."

"Probably," I reply. "But just one."

"Do you want me to pretend I'm mad at you so you can have an Oreo, too?" Ellie smiles over her shoulder and winks at me like someone much older—like a big sister who has just returned from college with a swollen brain full of special insights.

I am mulling over Ellie's proposition, my fingers dangling from the cliff of my knees, when suddenly Aloysius appears in the doorway. There isn't any warning or time to prepare. He lunges for me, his bright teeth bared, this tiny dog with a red-ribboned neck whose image so often bedecks quilts and guest towels, anything patterned in plaid.

Before Ellie can rescue me, her dog has peeled back the skin on the middle finger of my right hand. I am gushing warm and red in amazement—the pain has yet to arrive—while I struggle at the same time to staunch the spurting blood with my one splayed palm. If Ellie's mother is anything like mine, she mustn't find stains on the light-colored linoleum.

"I don't know what's wrong," Ellie keeps saying as she ushers me into the bathroom, the apron strings straining at her neck and breasts. "My mother said if he did it again, he'd have to be put down. You're not going to tell, are you? Promise me you aren't going to tell."

She holds my hand over the sink and rummages through the medicine cabinet for a bottle of rubbing alcohol. "This will clean the wound," Ellie promises. As she pours the clear liquid over my finger, my whole body jolts in dismay, then regret. The sound of this pain is a soprano screeching off-key. Dizzy and sobbing, I slump back against the wall, my hand shaking now beyond my control, as Ellie wraps a bandage. "If you could just hold still," she says. "I know I can make this good as new in no time. Please, Julie, promise me you won't tell."

Despite my protests that I am feeling fine now and my gratitude for the peace offering of Oreos, Ellie insists on walking me home. I think this is because she doesn't truly believe I will keep my mouth shut about how my hand got hurt, but I need her to keep her mouth shut about how we were playing unsupervised at her house and how I have eaten enough cookies to spoil my appetite for dinner tonight and the rest of the week.

"Just in time," my father says, pushing open the screen door. "Your mother and I were beginning to worry."

"Hello, Mr. Wade," Ellie chimes.

"Oh, Ellie, hello. I didn't see you there."

"It's kind of hard to miss me," she grins, gesturing to her tie-dyed T-shirt and jean shorts. "There's just so much of me to see."

This making jokes at her own expense is something Ellie only seems to do when she is nervous, and I can see that she is nervous now. Little beads of sweat dapple the baby hairs along her temples, those soft, white wisps not long enough or thick enough to be pulled back into a French or fishtail braid.

"Yes, well, it is dinnertime," my father says, his voice trailing off, and this is when he notices my enormous, mummified finger. "Julie, what happened there?"

"Oh, that," I say dismissively. "It's nothing really. I snagged my knuckle on a rosebush."

"A *pink* rosebush," Ellie clarifies. I shoot her a sharp look. *Doesn't she get that I prefer to work alone?*

"Well, all the same, I think your mother better have a look at it."

"Mr. Wade, we were playing in the garden, and I've been scratched up by rosebushes many times, so I knew just what to do. I cleaned Julie's finger, and I made a splint, and she'll be good as new in no time."

"Thank you, Ellie, but I think you should run along now. You girls will see each other again soon, I'm sure."

Ellie flashes me a look that says *Don't kill my dog!* as she turns back toward the street and lopes slowly away. Once inside the house, my mother is summoned, and despite the throbbing in my finger, I plead that nothing hurts at all, that nothing really happened. "We were just playing, and I crashed into a rosebush. Besides, I'm starving," I lie. "What's for dinner?"

"If it's just a little scratch," my mother says, "why didn't you use a little Band-Aid?"

"The Bigelows didn't have any more. They only had surgical tape and the big cloth kind." Lies are like iguanas, I realize, the way they just keep growing to fit the room.

"Let me see it," my mother demands, grabbing my wrist and pulling me into the bathroom. "Bill, check on the soup, will you?"

When my mother unwraps my finger, I know all hope of a credible alibi has crumbled. She looks from my face to my shredded skin and back again in the portentous silence just before a tea kettle squeals. "Do you want to tell me again that this is from a rosebush?" she says, following a long, dramatic pause.

I don't answer.

"It has to hurt," she appraises. "I would imagine it hurts so bad you can hardly stand it."

"Not really." I keep my head down and try not to look at the cross section of my own flesh. Seeing the skin pulled away from the bone that way makes the throbbing so much worse.

"Looks to me like something with teeth did this. What do you think?"

"Thorns—from a rosebush," I reply through tight lips with my teeth clamped behind them.

"Bill, come in here please! I'd like to get your opinion on something." My dad, who doesn't have a strong stomach, takes one look at my finger and starts dry-heaving over the sink.

"Julie, what in the world—is that a dog bite?" He holds a towel to his mouth and tries only to meet my eyes.

"I'm calling Trudy Bigelow," my mother announces.

"Don't do it! Please! Ellie says they'll put Aloysius down!"

She doesn't even bother to turn around and shout "Aha!" My mother is already dialing Trudy's number from the French phone on her nightstand.

"Yes, Ellie I'd like to speak to your mother please . . . Mrs. Wade . . . Oh, she isn't? I see. What about your father? . . . I see." I slump on the toilet seat and let my head fall down between my legs. "Well, tell Trudy to call me the *instant* she gets home." The blood is rushing to my head, swishing around in my ears like a waterfall. When I wake, I'm lying on my parents' bed, limbs splayed like a starfish, and they are peering down at me the way we peer at creatures that wash up on the shore.

"First, we're going to take you to the doctor," my mother snaps the moment she sees my eyes flutter. "Then, we're going to talk about your punishment."

Over the next few days, news began to trickle down to me in increments. The first good news was that I didn't need a shot because Ellie's dog, though clearly suffering from some kind of human-directed rage, had received all his checkups and required vaccinations. The first bad news was that Ellie had been barred from the family kitchen for a full week as punishment for trying to deceive my parents as well as her own. I pictured her in the great chamber of her bedroom, shuffling Tarot cards, eating cookie dough, and staring out the window.

The next good news was that my finger, which Dr. Kumasaka had promised would heal, was also likely to heal with a scar. Since scars were a million times better than freckles or moles, serving as maps toward the treasure of a story, I reveled in the prospect of my future tattoo, a white, jagged line striking like lightning just below my cuticle. I laid awake nights as my finger itched itself whole, waiting for that grand blemish—marking both transgression and survival—to form.

The next bad news, however, was that I would have to pay for my scar with yard work. "You lied to us, and you broke the rules, and since you claimed it was a rosebush that started it all"—my mother handed me a pair of gloves and a three-pronged trowel—"it seems only fitting that we should send you out to weed around the roses."

"Can I keep the fallen petals for potpourri?" I asked, hopeful, knowing Alicia had already procured some mesh-net for sachets.

"Stick to your task," my mother said, her voice harsh, a little lipstick smudged across her teeth. "No daydreaming. For once in your life, just do as you're told." It went without saying that I wouldn't see Ellie again for a while.

But then, as I was trying to make a hexagon of rocks in the rich, moist soil—*or should it have been a pentagon? I couldn't remember what Ellie said witches' sacred symbol was*—I peered through the lattice of our fence and watched a brown, braided head bobbing along behind it, a body army-crawling through the grass. Ellie's face was streaked with tears, but she made the wise choice to dress in earth tones and not to move too fast.

"Don't say anything," she whispered. "I'm sure you're being watched."

"Always," I lamented without looking back.

"My mom just took Aloysius to the death vet."

"I didn't—"

"Shhh! I told you not to talk. Anyway, it's not your fault . . . *entirely*. Aloysius bit Brian this morning, and then he broke his lava lamp, and that was the last straw."

"I'm sorry."

"My dad didn't come home to say good-bye. I'm not even sure my mom told him, and we aren't allowed to call without permission."

"So, what are you going to do?" I started dramatically digging up some weeds to give the impression that I was working hard to earn my keep.

"Once I get back in the kitchen," Ellie resolved, her small nose cherry-red with ire, "I'm going to learn how to make those desserts that flame, and then I'm going to burn that whole house down."

I never saw Tim Bigelow again, and I don't think Ellie or Brian did either. They said good-bye to Aloysius when Trudy strapped the muzzle on and carted him away in the back seat of her bright green Nova. Tim and Trudy had matching cars. Trudy's was green, and Tim's was red, and sitting together on the drive, they looked like Christmas. It had been a long time since Christmas.

One day in early summer, Trudy came over to the house, and Ellie was suddenly welcomed inside as if nothing had happened. We were told to help ourselves to diet Frescas in the basement fridge and then to play a game on my brand-new Nintendo. Just the day before my dad had told me that if I wanted to play with Ellie Bigelow, it had to be active games—like tennis in the street or bike-riding around the neighborhood. "Dimples in the face are fine," he smiled, patting my head, "but we can't have you getting dimples in your arms and knees, now can we?"

Before long, Ellie had the Betty Crocker frosting open, and we were eating it in huge spoonfuls while she took the role of Mario and I followed behind as Luigi, collecting coins and leaping over mushrooms. Upstairs, Trudy told my mother about the impending divorce, about the money she had saved and the money she was going to demand.

"It wasn't a real marriage anyway. He wanted the kids. He wanted the life in the suburbs with the house and the yard. For too long, I just went along for the ride."

I never knew until afterwards—after the sirens had faded into the warm night, after the news reports when my parents made me clean my already-immaculate room—that the same day Ellie Bigelow and I ate a whole tub of dark chocolate cake frosting and advanced to Super Mario Brothers level 6 without once calling the hotline for assistance, Tim Bigelow was busy down at the Fauntleroy Community Church, making a noose and securing the rope around one of the tall, sturdy, evergreen trees. Ellie had been telling me how she thought she would hold a séance and try to contact Aloysius. Dogs might have voices on the Other Side, she mused. Tim left a note for Trudy that read, "YOU DID THIS TO ME," and she found him dangling there at the appointed meeting place—in his grass-stained jeans and his flannel shirt, despite the fact that it was June. He must have smelled of peat and roses, the garden dirt still caked under his fingernails. I pictured them cutting him down like a large, gray-haired flower, sad and broken but maybe perennial somehow. I closed my eyes and wished as hard as I could—that Tim Bigelow would blossom on the Other Side; that there really was an Other Side at all.

"Aren't you going to the funeral?" I ask Aunt Linda.

"I already sent flowers," she replies. "Mine was the first bouquet."

"A lovely arrangement," says Grandma June, who is making coffee and setting the table for three. "There were calla lilies and sweet peas, baby's breath and some light pink peonies—"

"Until your mother took credit for it." Linda looks into my eyes, and for the first time, I doubt her faith in me and in our unswerving alliance.

My lower lip quivers. "What do you mean?"

"Just a misunderstanding," Grandma soothes. "And I'm sure the other Linda has also sent flowers, dear."

"She brought some," I say. "My mother brought flowers from our garden to the service today."

"Cheap as ever," Aunt Linda retorts. "But she doesn't mind soaking up the praise when someone else is footing the bill." I watch as she collects her orange peels in a newspaper, then pitches them in the trash before disappearing down the hall.

"What happened?" I ask. "Is Aunt Linda mad at me? Did I do something wrong?"

"No, dear. People sometimes get a little testy where matters of death are concerned."

"I'm not *testy*, Mama!" Linda calls from the next room.

"I'll finish making these cube steak sandwiches, and everyone will sit down to lunch and forget all this nonsense," Grandma promises.

"My parents wouldn't let me go to the funeral. They said funerals are no place for children—but Ellie and Brian are there."

"Well, he was their father." Grandma fries the cube steaks now, square patties of bright pink meat, while holding something that looks like a fly swatter over the skillet's edge.

"What's that?"

"A splatter guard. It keeps the hot grease from leaping out of the pan." For a moment, I think of Ellie and her fantasy revenge of cherries jubilee or baked Alaska. Then, I wonder if you have to capitalize the "A" in "Alaska." *If it's not a state, is it still a proper noun?*

"Grandma, I have a question."

"Yes?" She is busy laying out pieces of Wonder Bread and hands me Kraft singles, tomato slices, and French's mustard to do the trimmings.

"Is Mrs. Bigelow still Mrs. Bigelow now that her husband died?"

"Well, I'm still Mrs. Wade, and my husband died."

"But Grandpa didn't kill himself," I argue. "He didn't *choose* to leave. Mr. Bigelow did."

"A name is a gift, dear. Parents give their children the gift of a first name, and husbands give their wives the gift of a last name. Gifts can't be taken back, and I think most folks are of the mind that they shouldn't be given back either."

"What if they had gotten divorced? Would Trudy get her name back then?" I lower my voice now the way my mother does when imparting scandalous information: "Because, you know, that's where Tim and Trudy Bigelow were headed."

"Where?"

"*Splitsville.*" I say it with bravado, the way Punky Brewster would.

My grandmother looks at me, startled and a touch disappointed, too, like I have just taken the Lord's name in vain.

"Go tell your aunt that lunch is ready. And"—she turns off the stove and wipes her hands clean—"let's have some lighter conversation, shall we?"

Aunt Linda's childhood room is small and stuffy as a cracker box with a narrow dresser and a single bed and one long, skinny window no good for climbing out of. It does have a new blue carpet, though, and a closet door with a clicky handle and a full-length mirror on the outside.

"Lunch is ready," I say, tapping tentatively on the door.

"I'll be there in a minute."

"Grandma says we have to talk about light things at lunch, but maybe afterwards—would you like me to try to read your palm?"

"I'm not sure Jesus would approve," Linda replies. Then, conceding: "But maybe, in a little while."

She is sitting cross-legged on the floor beside her bed like a much younger person. Her back is to me and the door, as she shuffles a stack of pictures like playing cards.

"What are those pictures of?" I ask.

"Oh, just some snapshots from my college days."

I kneel on the bed and peer over her shoulder. It's a black-and-white print of Aunt Linda in a grass skirt standing by a bonfire. Her feet are bare, as is her smooth midriff and her slender arms. She wears pigtails with a white flower tucked in each one.

"You look happy," I say. I realize that, in real life, I have rarely seen such joyful serenity ease the creases of my aunt's tight face.

"This was on Oahu," she says. "That's Waikiki Beach, and—hiding behind me—see that girl standing there?"

I squint to make out a pair of Bermuda shorts and a face blurred in motion.

"That's Trudy Bigelow. She always hated having her picture taken. She always said she'd rather have the thousand words."

"What was Trudy's last name before she married Tim?"

"Oh, it was—now isn't that silly? Of course I know what her name was. We knew each other for years . . ."

"It's OK," I say. "It's OK if you can't remember. Grandma is waiting for us."

"It starts with an 'N,' I think. Come on. What's her mother's name? Mrs.—" I stand beside Aunt Linda and offer her a hand. "It'll come to me," she insists. "For goodness sake, it hasn't been *that* many years."

And because I am a budding philosopher as well as an accomplished sleuth, I have to ask her, "Do you think maybe you can't remember because the Trudy she was doesn't exist anymore?" I am conjuring the teal pantsuit now, the thick rouge and lined lips, the sharp, cold eyes that stared right into the lens as if beseeching, *Look at me, that's right, look at me.*

"Don't be ridiculous," Aunt Linda chides, still keeping her distance as we move toward the kitchen. "And please, don't put words in my mouth."

Mrs. Magnussen

[Or a Study of Desire That Doesn't Cover All the Bases]

If it had been possible in those days to make a grown woman your friend, I would have chosen Mrs. Magnussen first among the mothers. It would have saved a lot of trouble, too, since much of the time I spent with her son Lee was an attempt to get closer to her—to learn her real first name (which wasn't *Mrs.*—it never is), and the contents of her kitchen drawers, and to hear her speak about what it meant to be the only woman in a house of men.

In the Magnussen house on Belvidere Street, there was one father—as there often is—who was small for a man, though more like a point guard than a jockey. He always wore shorts with tall socks and a loose polo shirt and drove a jeep I greatly admired. Mr. Magnussen, whose given name was Ronald, had a mustache he groomed with a tiny comb and cigarettes he smoked with a great deal of relish. I watched him pacing and puffing the length of the porch or sitting down with the paper, absently flicking his ash. *Did he not know— had no one told him—that smoking was a "filthy habit" and "only one step away from a sin"?*

Perhaps, when I thought about it, Mr. Magnussen had not yet met my mother.

There were two sons who lived in the house, both taller than their father but made in his image. Ronnie, by the time I knew him, was in sixth grade and had already dated at least a dozen girls. He liked to wear baseball jerseys and a cap turned sideways. He also had a mustache just as bushy as his father's and could buy cigarettes at the mini-mart without being asked for ID. That's how old he looked. The first time Lee brought me home, Ronnie sprawled face-down on the sofa in the living room, his feet flexed and hanging over the edge, while attempting to resuscitate the limp, pale body of the red-haired girl beneath him.

"Is this a CPR class?" I asked.

"They're making out," Lee said, as if it was obvious. "That's what you're supposed to do when you're in sixth grade."

We were in fourth grade, and I hadn't yet imagined what *we* were supposed to do.

"This is my mom," Lee announced as we entered the kitchen. She was a chubby woman with dark, curly hair and a sweet expression that suggested she was soft on punishments. She also had flour on the front of her dress and a rolling pin sticking out of her pocket.

"Oh, please excuse the mess!" Mrs. Magnussen exclaimed. "It's bake-sale season, and I'm up to my ear lobes in sugar cookies and Bundt cakes."

Lee fished around in the fridge and found us some Cokes, then kissed her cheek and told her we would be upstairs.

"And your name, dear?"

"It's Julie," I said, and despite my general aversion to the kitchen, the words came tumbling out. "Maybe I could help you with your baking." Then, glancing back at Lee: "Maybe we both could."

"Well, I appreciate the offer," she said, "but I'm sure you and Lee have better things to do than melt butter and mix dough."

"Oh, we don't mind," I pledged, remembering that my mother often spoke on behalf of her husband—on behalf of her whole family, in fact. She called it "the royal we," then laughed sternly (a hard thing to do), and my father and I were forced to go along. I rolled up my sleeves and put out my hands and waited for Mrs. Magnussen to adjust the faucet.

When I am honest with myself, which is not too often, I realize that part of my perennial desire to help Mrs. Magnussen in her kitchen was fueled by my even greater desire to avoid being alone with Lee in his bedroom. Ever since we skated hand-in-hand at the year's first roller-skating party, I got the sense that Lee was grooming me to be his girlfriend. I felt like his ticklish little mustache, twitching beneath the comb, waiting to be trimmed into new fashion.

"Did you know Ronnie had his first girlfriend when he was in third grade?" Lee brags as we head toward his house after school. "He's been all the way to third base—and I mean third base more than once."

"Is that why he always wears a baseball jersey?"

"No." Lee sighs and stops to pick dandelions out of the parking strip, then pops their golden heads off as we stroll along. "Don't you know about the bases?"

"I missed softball tryouts last year, but I know basically how the game works." When I played in the park, I did tend to use my own rules.

"Well, they're not the real bases anyway. They're the dating ones—the steps you go through if you really like somebody."

I'm not sure I like Lee enough yet to hear him explain.

"See, you have to start with kissing because that's first base, and if you don't kiss first, it's like you never even hit the ball."

"So, what are you saying?" I ask, feeling my throat tighten and the air in my lungs push all the way down to my stomach.

"I'm saying"—Lee turns to look at me with his big, hazel eyes and his long eyelashes that make him almost pretty, almost like a girl— "I'm just saying"—with a deep sigh—"you have to stop helping my mom so much in the kitchen."

Behind us, the yellow trail of flowers stretches back for a block or more. I look from Lee to the path and then to Lee's pert thumb, which is slick with lighters and also this—the prodigious beheading of blossoms.

"Now there's plenty of string cheese and snickerdoodles," Mrs. Magnussen says, reaching for her purse and keys, "so help yourself to whatever sounds good. I have to run to the grocery, and your father's resting in the den. Oh—and Ronnie's entertaining his girl-friend in the living room, so do your best not to bother them."

Entertaining? My mother wouldn't let me have a tea party in our living room.

Almost at once Lee takes my hand and leads me up the stairs, his palm so slick with perspiration I have to pry my own hand away and wipe it on my pants. "This is it," he beams, closing the door behind us. It is a cramped room with sloped ceilings and an overflowing hamper and a waterbed pressed against the window.

"Doesn't Elise Paul live next door to you?" I ask, raising the blinds.

"Yeah, I think so. Why?"

"I just like her name, that's all. It makes me think of Meg Ryan. I wish I had a girl's name *and* a boy's name."

"I think Wade can be a boy's name," Lee replies, growing weary of our small talk and starting to pace in little circles like his father. "Altoid?" He passes me the tin.

"That's OK. They're too strong for me."

Lee shoves three into his mouth and chews them quickly. "If we lie down on my bed, we can shoot baskets," he says, and I see that he has pinned a basketball hoop to the back of his door. There is no getting out now, so I take one of the Nerf balls and toss it toward the net for luck. Lee stretches out beside me on the twin bed and offers to take off my shoes.

"OK," I consent—"but I'm keeping my *socks* on."

The thing about Lee Magnussen that becomes perfectly clear in the first two seconds is that he only wants to impersonate his brother. He doesn't have any real moves of his own, but I'm a girl so I've been told I'm supposed to let the boy make the first one. Even if it is clumsy. Even if the boy reeks of bad grown-man cologne and Dep hair gel and Altoids that are still too strong in his mouth, let alone mine. Lee's kisses turn from salty and dry to sloppy and wet, but mostly he presses the weight of his whole body against me so my breath comes in little gasps. These are not the pleasure-sounds of ladies in the movies, though, the ones who stretch their fishnet-stockinged legs toward the ceiling while clasping their lovers' torsos with their red claw-nails.

Fearing suffocation, I turn my face to the side at windowsill level and gaze across the space between the two brick houses with the bright red trim. In her bedroom, Elise Paul hugs the hump of her knees beneath her harvest sweater. She talks on a phone with a curly cord that seems to stretch on forever. Suddenly, I wish this were my room in my house—that Lee and his father and brother didn't live here at all, though I would keep his mother—and then Elise Paul and I could send messages to each other with flashlights after dark in Morse code.

The next day at school, Carl Lulls presses his binder into my back so hard that I crash forward into a cluster of popular girls. They turn to flash me one collective scowl.

"What'd you do that for?"

"To get your attention," he smirks.

"Well, you've got it. What do you want?"

"I want to know why you didn't go all the way with Lee Magnussen last night. He says you two barely got to second base."

"It's none of your business," I retort, then grab his arm and pull him back into the alcove near the water fountain. "What does *all the way* mean? All the way to . . . *where?*"

Carl's mischievous grin slowly fades, and his brow furrows a little.

"I don't know, but Ronnie's been there, and Lee wanted to take you there, too. He said you were squirming a lot and staring out the window and then made some excuse about going to the bathroom, and he waited a long time, but you never came back."

"I couldn't help it," I say, my own palms turning slick in my pockets. "Mrs. Magnussen came home, and she needed help making cookies. She let me add the vanilla because she knows that's my favorite part."

"Rosemary's really nice and all," Carl concedes, "but at the end of the day, Lee's the one you're dating." *Were we dating? Was it official?*

"Carl!" I tug his arm before he barrels into the classroom, always walking hard and whistling, always calling attention to himself.

"What? We're gonna get in trouble, and I already have my name on the board."

I peer into his face like a seeker before an oracle—cautious, hopeful, and a little afraid. "Just tell me—is Mrs. Magnussen's name really *Rosemary?*"

I know I should be thinking of Lee Magnussen and of the love letters he has written to me with mechanical pencil on Steno paper in his most controlled cursive. He folds the letters into complex triangles that I struggle to unwrap, study in the cloakroom, stuff in my shoe, and later stow away in the Raggedy Ann planter on the nightstand in my room. But instead of what I should be thinking, I am lying in bed imagining Rosemary Magnussen in her kitchen. *Rosemary. Rose Mary.* It was two women's names pushed together into one, and who better than Rosemary Magnussen to embody this twofold femininity? *Rose,* a seductive flower with intricate folds and blooms. *Mary,* the blessed mother, who loved her son enough to let him go.

Rosemary. Rosemary. A loveseat of a name. Late into the night, I repeat it like the rosary Catholic kids recite, my hand dangling loose in the darkness, longing for something to hold.

At Christmastime, Mrs. Magnussen takes Lee and me downtown so she can do her shopping and we can appreciate the grand gold star beaming from the Bon Marche building. Inside the store, Lee walks confidently up to the counter and asks if he can see some of the rings glittering beneath the glass. The man in charge asks him if he is looking to buy or browse, and Lee says he's interested in the layaway program.

"What's that?" I whisper.

"You'll see." The male clerk confers with a female clerk who comes over to attend to us. The slit in her chest is so deep that her pearls stick in the middle, and she smells of fruit you wouldn't want to eat and is dusty all over with powder.

"How may I help you, young man?" she coos.

"I want to buy a ring for my girlfriend," Lee says. She turns to me now, and I gasp. Minus the tentacles and the suction cups, she looks exactly like Ursula the Sea Witch.

"Well, that's lovely, dear. And what is your price range?"

"I make five dollars a week," he says, "but my dad's going to increase my allowance to ten after New Year's."

I gasp again. "I make *one* dollar a week and do *tons* of chores. I've never seen you lift a finger!"

Ursula murmurs something about how a woman's work is never done and tells me I shouldn't get my hopes up because the world is slow to change. I nod politely, all the while studying Lee who is studying a gold band with a diamond shaped like a flower.

"How much is that one?" he asks.

"That's one-hundred-forty-nine ninety-nine," Ursula replies.

Lee rocks back on his heels the way I've seen my father do, jingling the coins in his pocket. "Can I put it on layaway? I have five dollars to put down today, and I can pay five dollars a week until I own it."

The ring is garish, too big for my taste and likely too big for my hand. Besides, I know I prefer silver (my mother insists "platinum"), but most of all, I like a colorful stone.

"You really don't have to buy me a ring," I say. "I'd be just as happy with a pocket knife." *Happier*—though I have heard diamonds can cut glass.

"It's OK," he assures me, pulling back his wallet's Velcro seal. "I want to. I want you to know I'm serious about you." We have already made each other friendship rings, and Lee has given me his ID bracelet to wear. We have had another kiss—our first good one—under the hallway mistletoe. We have even drained a Big Gulp together using only one straw.

"I know," I whisper, hoping Ursula will go away. "I know you're serious—but that's a lot of money, and who knows who we'll be by the time you pay it off."

Lee stares into my face sadly, wounded, his eyes more brown than green today and still as pretty as a girl's. Ursula is about to tell him how he needs to put down 25 percent of the total purchase now, which is close to forty dollars—a sum he doesn't have. Rosemary is about to return from perusing the neckties and handbags and buying a shawl for Lee's grandmother who lives someplace that is always cold with a furnace that cuts in and out. The adults are about to put an end to all his best-laid plans, but it is clear that I am the one who has really disappointed him.

"I would have married you," Lee says, his voice low and cold. "We could have gotten engaged and everything. Now, as things are, you'll probably end up with a Whitman Sampler in your stocking."

I squeeze his hand and smile hard, harder than I feel. "But you know how much I like chocolate."

"So, are you and Lee Magnussen breaking up?" Carl Lull follows me into the single-stall bathroom near the pottery room.

"You can't be in here. I'll tell Mrs. Miller."

"It's a girl *and* a boy bathroom, for one thing, and I'm already in Time Out, so there's not much more they can do to me."

Carl has a point.

"How can we be breaking up if I wasn't even sure we were going out to begin with?" I pump the soap into my dry hands and study the small granules that won't turn to foam unless I add water. It is becoming more and more apparent that everything is also something else.

"I don't know," Carl shrugs, "but grown-ups do it all the time."

"I didn't mean to hurt his feelings," I say, suddenly panicked, like maybe Lee is the only shot I'll ever have at love and now I've gone and ruined everything. "What can I do to make it up to him?"

"You know what you can do." Carl sounds older now. His voice deepens as he leans against the sink, one hand propped against the wall.

"Do I?"

"Guys don't want you to tell them how you feel. They want you to *show* them." Now he hoists his heavy backpack over his shoulder and turns toward the door.

"Carl, have you been through all the bases yet?"

"Yeah," he says, "lots of times." But I'm not sure I believe him.

"Who with?"

He looks back, cocks his head, and stares at the paper towel dispenser, which is empty and has never worked right anyway. "Just this girl," he says. "You don't know her."

In the New Year, we learn about palindromes, which are words, phrases, or numbers that read the same in regular or backwards order. The New Year itself is a palindrome (1991), which Mrs. Miller says is *serendipitous,* a word I love, though I'm still not exactly sure what it means. Some girls have palindromes for names, like Eve or Hannah, and some boys too, like Bob or Otto. For homework, we have to choose a phrase that is or incorporates a palindrome and bring it to class with colored or collaged illustrations. I plan to use *fall leaves as leaves fall* since autumn is my favorite season and since Grandma June has already given me a stencil that will make my leaves look better than any free-hand drawing could. Then, I'll write a story to bring the phrase to life.

At Lee Magnussen's house, we set out our work on the dining room table, and Rosemary brings us each a glass of milk. "You can put strawberry Quik in it if you want," she smiles, patting my arm. "I'll be in the other room tending the babies."

For extra money, the Magnussens are opening a daycare center in their home. Since the living room is headquarters, Ronnie has to take his dates to the basement now, where Lee says there is a couch that folds out into a bed and also a pool table and a punching bag. I'm especially interested in the punching bag, but we aren't allowed to go down there because of Ronnie's privacy.

"What palindrome did you choose?" I ask Lee, not caring much but trying to make conversation. Things have been tense between us, but Lee hasn't demanded his ID bracelet back yet.

"It's not important," he replies, snipping pictures from some sleek-looking magazine.

"I figure most of the boys will choose *Madam, I'm Adam.*"

"Not me," he says. "My dad knew a much better one that isn't on the list."

"Can I see?"

"I'll show you when it's finished," Lee agrees.

We work in silence awhile, and Rosemary never comes to check on us, even though I am always hoping she will. When I finish sketching the tree and shading all the stenciled leaves in different autumn tones, I proudly print my name in the top right corner and turn the page around so Lee can see.

"What do you think?"

"It's nice," he says without really looking up.

"Can I see yours now?"

Lee is busy with a brush and a jar of rubber cement, but he doesn't tell me I can't peek at his pictures. In block letters with a black Sharpie, he has printed the palindrome: *Girl, bathing on Bikini, eyeing boy, sees boy eyeing bikini on bathing girl.* Beneath it, he has pasted the body of a woman in a skimpy, two-piece swimsuit with sand smeared all over her chest. She is stretched out on her side with the ocean creeping up behind, and in the distance, a lifeguard with red swim trunks and a shiny, hairless chest strides toward her. I can just make out the tiny, silver whistle in his mouth.

"Wow," I say, "that's serendipitous."

"No." Lee flashes me a satisfied smile. "That's *Sports Illustrated*, the best magazine in the whole world. My dad got Ronnie a subscription for Christmas."

We stand eyeing each other for some time and listening to the babies cry. So far Rosemary only has two clients—baby Katie and baby Angela—but she is hopeful that business will pick up soon.

"Do you want to have a pillow fight in my parents' room?" Lee ventures. His thin real mustache is camouflaged by a thick milk mustache, but his fingernails are trim and clean, which my father says is a mark of good grooming. The woman in the white bikini seems to blink at me in Morse code: *What are you waiting for?*

"OK," I say—"but I'm keeping my socks on."

When spring comes, we spend more time outdoors, which takes me away from Rosemary's kitchen but also keeps me out of Lee's bedroom. I recognize this as a compromise, which my mother describes as a situation where nobody gets what they want. She prefers to have her own way and so avoids compromises altogether, but my father says compromise is inevitable, so I better get used to it.

Lee offers me his old bicycle because he is going to ride his brother's new one. It is taller than Lee's and has hand brakes and about a dozen more important gears. I don't mind, though, because Lee's bike is orange, and orange is emerging as my newest favorite color. We both fasten helmets under our chins and race off toward the Holy Rosary Playground, which is closest to his house. On the way, Lee dares me to take the curbs instead of the sidewalk ramps, saying those are mostly for strollers and old ladies with walkers or grocery carts. For awhile, I match him jump for jump, lifting out of my seat long enough to sail over the curb, then thumping down hard as I land. The place between my legs—the place there is no name for—begins to throb by the time we pass through the cyclone fence and crest over the concrete hill.

I think of words I have learned that are especially pleasurable on the tongue.

Palindrome. Serendipity. Imagine saying these words aloud: *My palindrome hurts* or *My serendipity is sore.* Then, I think of Rosemary, waving to us from the window, a cloth diaper over her shoulder and baby Angela asleep in her arms.

When I open my eyes, Lee Magnussen and Carl Lull are standing over me, their faces pinched tight by the black straps of their helmets. For a moment, I think of a story my mother told me about the boys who used to chase her home from school, pin her down on the pavement, then take turns kissing her while she screamed.

"I bet you hated it," I said, genuinely sorry for her pain.

"No, no," she volunteered, with a wistful look in her eyes. "I enjoyed the attention. But a girl should never let on that she likes it, or she'll end up with a bad reputation."

"What happened?" There is a faint ringing in my ears that may or may not be church bells.

"You flipped off the bike," Lee says, more impressed than concerned. "Carl saw you, and he went to get my mother. She'll be here in a minute with the car."

"The jeep?" I ask, hopeful.

"No, the wagon. My dad's working overtime."

"Oh."

"Did you do it on purpose?" Carl wants to know. "Because if you did, you're some kind of crazy, kamikaze rock star."

Kamikaze. I like this word, too. By now, *my kamikaze is killing me.*

Just then, Rosemary arrives on the scene with her horn blaring. She has both babies strapped into car seats and leaves the motor running as she leaps out of the car. "Oh, Julie, oh, dear, are you all right? . . . Back away, boys. Give me some room."

She kneels beside me with her first aid kit that looks like a little red suitcase perfect for one of Santa's traveling elves. "What hurts? Can you tell me what hurts?"

"My knees, I guess—and my chin." She leans over me now, and I catch a whiff of her hairspray, which smells like roses. *How perfect*, I smile.

Rosemary has large, brown eyes that peer into my face and light creases where she smiles. I have never seen Lee's mother this close before, and when she rolls up my pant leg and touches my skin, I startle.

"I'm sorry. Did I hurt you?" She winces with empathy.

"No." I shake my head. "You didn't hurt me."

Rather, when Rosemary Magnussen touches me, all the little blond hairs on my arms and legs stand erect like attentive soldiers. As she cleans and dresses my wounds with strange white Band-Aids that open like doves, a sharp, electric feeling courses from my head to my heels. I have never felt anything like it before, not even when Lee Magnussen took my ear lobe between his teeth the way his brother told him girls especially like. Not even at the end of a pillow fight.

"Best of all," she smiles, cupping my cheek, "I don't think any of this is going to leave a scar."

The real serendipity is that, due to my gashes and my tender back, I am banned from any more "roughhousing" for a while. Lee mopes around the house with a fruit roll-up and a copy of *GQ*, and I return triumphantly to the kitchen.

"Are you this helpful to your mother at home?" Mrs. Magnussen asks.

I tell her the truth. "Not really. My mother doesn't trust me much in the kitchen."

"That's a shame, dear. You're a natural." I'm not, but I've decided to let her believe this is true. "And tonight I'm making rosemary chicken."

"Named after you!" I exclaim, dreaming at once of a Julie flan or a Julie torte or a flaming Julie's jubilee.

"Well, not exactly. But it does involve my namesake." She takes down a little glass bottle from the spice rack. I trace the garish cursive with my hand. *Rosemary*.

"Rosemary is an herb?" I say, not believing. "I thought it was a compound word."

"I guess it's that, too," she smiles, hands to my waist as she slides me further down the counter and out of her way.

"So," to clarify, "you're *not* named after Rose and Mary?"

"Who are they?"

"Some kind of great enchantress, I assume—and the famous virgin mother."

She laughs aloud and opens a can of bread crumbs. "Hardly. I think, if anything, I'm named after my mother's favorite spice."

"Oh, that's nice," I say. "I'm named after Julie Andrews. *Sort of.*"

"Is that a fact?" Rosemary smiles. It isn't, but I've decided I want it to be. "I just love *The Sound of Music.*" She hands me the cooking spray.

"So did my parents. They went to see it thirteen times when they were dating."

"Really? That's amazing." If she doesn't believe me, she is an even better liar than I am.

"Now I think for dessert I'm going to make some good, old-fashioned chocolate brownies. How does that sound?"

"Yes," I sigh, summoning my martyr's voice. "I wish I could have chocolate brownies sometimes."

"Well, of course you can, dear. Call your parents. See if you can stay for dinner."

"Oh, it isn't that," I explain, completely enthralled in this story and growing more confident as I speak. "You see, I'm allergic to chocolate. If I eat it, I get really sick. The doctors say if I eat too much, I could die."

For some reason when I lie to Mrs. Magnussen, all my hairs stand on end again, and the electric sensation from the playground returns. It's exciting—watching her respond with interest and concern, feeling her regard me as if I'm special, exceptional, set apart from the others by my name and dietary restrictions. When I lie, I become powerful. Mrs. Magnussen decides to make blueberry compote instead.

"Maybe I could stay for dinner after all."

Over the next few weeks, I have a built-in alibi to avoid pillow fights and other forms of wrestling with Lee. My knee hurts or my back aches or the bruises on my arms have yet to fully heal. He seems generally sullen and has started spending more time with Marissa Sheldon, but I don't mind because I have weekly cooking time with his mother. I have even started helping out with the children as her babysitting business begins to boom.

When the school year ends, Rhianna Blakely has a private party at her house on Concord Street. My parents won't permit me to attend because the invitation smells like smoke and Rhianna's father is a race car driver. (*Race car,* I note, is a palindrome.) Later, I hear through the grapevine that Lee played spin the bottle at Rhianna's party and made out with three, different girls.

Maybe this is how relationships end, I ponder. People just lose interest in each other. But then my mother says Mrs. Magnussen has called to invite us over to lunch. She says for me to bring my swimsuit so that Lee and I can run through the sprinklers if we want. It is almost July. My mother inspects my swimsuits, noting they are pilled and stretched out and faded from too much chlorine. "I'd be embarrassed to have you seen in these things," she sighs, then tows me off to Sears to make a new selection.

Mr. Magnussen is smoking on the porch when we arrive, and my mother's eyebrows arch so high she looks like St. Louis. "Go on in, ladies," he waves. "Rosie's setting up a picnic for you all out back."

Lee stands in the hallway punching his baseball glove. We barely acknowledge each other. My mother, still reeling from Mr. Magnussen's filthy habit, moves slowly toward the kitchen and out through the back door where a table has been arranged with cloth napkins and sparkling silverware.

"Linda, so nice to see you!" Mrs. Magnussen waves. "I'll put the teapot on, and the kids can cool off down there on the lawn." She points toward the oscillating sprinkler, then calls for Lee to come outside and be a better host.

"Would you like to change into your swimsuit, dear? You can use the powder room just there."

In the tiny bathroom, I lean against the sink and study my face in the mirror. It is always shiny now, even when I am not sweating. Along my temples and across my collarbones, the first acne rosettes have begun their ominous bud. Before long, this strange garden will spread like overgrowth around my nose and mouth. I sense the contagion coming but stand powerless in my altered skin.

Lee knocks on the door. "Just a minute," I say, the new two-piece still in my hand. The tags have not been cut yet, so it is not too late to return it. What did the palindrome say? *Girl, bathing on Bikini, eyeing boy, sees boy eyeing bikini on bathing girl.* I take a deep breath and allow myself to be exposed. The small, uneven bumps of my breasts don't fill out the cups, so I cinch the string tighter at my neck.

"Hurry up!" Lee says. "I have practice at three."

I walk across the sticky linoleum, arms knitted behind my back, head down. Both my mother and Mrs. Magnussen seem to inspect me as I step forward onto the patio, but even at this short distance, I can't make sense of their expressions. Lee brushes my shoulder as he passes, then casts back an approving smile. Still, the mothers haven't moved, and this is when I begin to realize that no matter what else may be true, Mrs. Magnussen is always a mother, and this will color her perception of me.

It is becoming more and more apparent that everything is also something else.

I adjust my straps again and step forward into the umbrella's shade. I notice a platter on the table with several chocolate cupcakes and a single lemon one. Lee notices at the same time and asks, "Who's that yellow cupcake for?"

But before anyone can answer, Mrs. Magnussen says "Shhh!" with the stern force of a librarian, then points to the portable radio. The faint ringing in my ears is definitely not church bells.

". . . The star, beloved by fans of *Bonanza, Little House on the Prairie,* and *Highway to Heaven,* died of cancer today at his home in Malibu. He was 54 years old."

"What is it? What happened?" I ask. I can see now that both mothers have tears in their eyes.

"It's the end of an era," my mother laments, then fishes for her compact inside her deep bag.

Lee stands beside me in his red swim trunks, his skinny chest flecked with new hairs and goose bumps. "Are we running through the sprinklers or not?"

"Show a little respect!" Rosemary commands. I have never seen her angry before. I could never have imagined it. "Both of you, sit down and keep your mouths shut." She holds the napkin up to her face so we can no longer see her as she weeps, "Michael Landon"—I am flipping through a rolodex of words, looking for one I can hold onto—"that beautiful, beautiful man has died."

But not a single word will hold me—not *serendipity,* not *rosemary,* nothing. There is nothing to say. An era has ended. I open my towel like a parachute, then wrap it tightly around my tentative skin.

Mrs. Williams

[Or a Study of Postmodernism and
the Many Ways That Walls Are Broken]

I have to be frank with you: this story won't end well, no matter how I tell it. If that's a deal-breaker, then you might want to quit while you're ahead, flip through a magazine instead, or find the best thing to watch on television.

Jenna Williams was a writer, and I was too, which brought us together in the beginning and set us apart at the end. It wasn't the writing exactly, you understand, but what we believed about it. Jenna always said, "There are some things you just can't write your way out of." If I had taken her word for it, I wouldn't be writing this now.

I met Jenna when she was in sixth grade and I was in seventh. I had skipped sixth grade at my old school to get out of a bad situation, but ironically, I ended up in a worse one at the Calvary Lutheran Church School on 35th Avenue. My mother loved a bargain, and, as it happened, she and my father had been shopping for a new church ever since my mother's unfortunate alienation of the entire congregation at our old church, St. Paul's of Shorewood Lutheran on 21st Avenue. Fourteen blocks was just far enough to make a fresh start in West Seattle, and it turned out, if you transferred your membership to Calvary, you could send a child to school there for 20 percent off. This is what they mean by "two birds with one stone."

The Williamses also may have joined the church for pecuniary reasons. They were a single-income family, since Mr. Williams didn't work outside the home, and the multichild discount surely proved appealing. Calvary was so desperate to boost enrollment at that time that you could educate two kids in church school for little more than the price of one. Tithing was expected of course, but my mother thought you could bring a Bundt cake to coffee hour and call it even. Who knows? Maybe the Williamses did, too.

That first Sunday was an exercise in hyperbole. My mother wore too many bangles and a straw hat swathed with gauzy, purple ribbon. I think she was going as Anne of the Island. She dressed my father in a burgundy sweater-vest and gray sport coat, even though it was August and sweat was pooling in the dent under everyone's nose. My ensemble was pink and trimmed with lace, a ruffled mistake my mother had snagged from the clearance rack at JCPenney's. "Glinda called; she wants her dress back," someone might have said, but, mercifully, no one was using that rhetorical construction yet.

From our place in last pew, I scanned the room of receding hairlines and elastic-waist pants, of walkers propped on tennis balls protruding into the aisles. For some reason, Lutheran seemed to be synonymous with old. Perhaps the Lutherans recruited so hard because their core contingent was dying off, and soon there would be no one left to light the candles or water the ferns or bake those obligatory Bundt cakes. But if these hymn-singing elders thought I was sticking around, they had another thing coming. Someday I'd make it to college, where rumor had it chapel was optional and nylons would become a scratchy relic of the past.

When I glanced over at the pew beside ours, I saw Jenna, a tall, sturdy girl with Barbie-blond hair and cheeks perpetually scorched—like she was always blushing and could never stop—giving me the once-over with her big, cornflower eyes. I bowed my head and pretended to read my bulletin. When I looked up again, she put her pointer finger to her temple and made the shape of a gun. As the organ music swelled to the top of the treble clef, she flicked her thumb and fired.

I liked Jenna instantly. She had the round, expressive face of a Disney character, impish and well-meaning at the same time. She was the sort of girl who would have been thoroughly believable as the plucky sidekick in a sitcom or film—the one who plays Janeane Garofalo to another girl's Meg Ryan; the one who doesn't believe she's as pretty as she really is, or sadly, as worthy of love.

Like all the girls I knew, Jenna also had a mother. For better or worse, there seemed no getting around this fact. Mrs. Williams was a short, svelte woman in tailored slacks who stood beside her daughter, holding the hymnal with a formal air but only mouthing the words. I admired her low investment in this task, the way she didn't seem out to impress anyone with gusto, feigned or otherwise. Mrs. Williams' hair had once been blond, too, I could tell, but it had since turned the color of ash and sand and was styled like Diane Keaton's in every movie since *Annie Hall*—which I wasn't allowed to watch, by the way, because my mother hated Woody Allen. I had seen the video case at the library plenty of times, though, and the fact was, Mrs. Williams looked a lot like Diane Keaton. If only she had worn the ties!

My eyes rolled over the Williams clan as though they were beads on an abacus. I had done this with my own family too, countless times, wanting us all to add up to something—a story that made sense. Jenna's brother was small and nondescript, Kieran Culkin in a white T-shirt and blue jeans. He knelt and slid his toy trucks along the pew, and his mother, who let him wear the T-shirt and jeans to begin with (*to church, of all places!* my mother would later shriek), also didn't force him to stand.

Mr. Williams towered above the rest of the family. I knew of no celebrity equivalent for him, except maybe Raymond Burr in the new *Perry Mason* made-for-TV movies. Not that he was as old as Raymond Burr, mind you, but similarly imposing and sad. His flesh seemed to fold into layers, and a thin, navy sweater stretched across his chest like a tent with a wide pole through the middle. The pants beneath him hung low and were belted to his torso in such a way that I could only imagine him tipping from side to side like a teapot, never moving forward or back. When the time came for communion, I noted that he did not join his family at the altar.

"So, do you go to the school, too, or just the church?" Jenna asks, cutting me in line for donut holes. By school, she means the portables in the parking lot where I have recently taken a series of exams to prove I am not too duncey to enroll in seventh grade.

"Starting next week," I say. "You?"

"Same." She crams as many donut holes into her cheeks as she can, which gives her the likeness of an embarrassed chipmunk or sunburned blowfish—a cartoon character either way. When she swallows at last, with an acoustic gulp, Jenna motions for me to follow her outside.

"What grade?"

"Seventh," I say.

Her rosy balloon-cheeks inflate again, and she sighs. "Really? You don't look the type."

"To be in seventh grade?"

"No, Silly—to be a delinquent. I'm Jenna, by the way." She takes a swig of watery fruit punch in a Dixie cup and sizes me up some more.

"A delinquent? I'm not a delinquent." *What delinquent ever dressed like the Good Witch of the North?* "I'm Julie," I tell her, and put out my hand.

Jenna slaps me five and continues. Maybe she thinks handshakes are for burly old men and tinny-voiced ladies. Maybe she's right. "Look, from what my parents told me, the seventh–eighth grade combination class is mostly for delinquents. They added the middle school just last year because so many kids in this part of town have been flunking out of public school. A lot of their parents and grandparents go to church here, so they figure it's a good market for rehabilitation."

"Well, how am I going to fit in with a bunch of delinquents?" I ask, half-rhetorically, gazing across the staggered rows of cars to the big, brown, architectural turd that is soon to become Matriculation Central.

"Oh, you're not," Jenna laughs, but there's no malice in it. She pokes her Birkenstocks through the gaps in the railing, wipes her hands on her paisley skirt. "It's no big deal," she promises. "I'm a misfit, too, so we'll look for each other at recess."

My parents assured me that Jenna Williams must have a fanciful imagination because there was no way on earth they would enroll any daughter of theirs in a delinquents' middle school, even to save a buck. Since I was their only daughter, I assumed they were telling the truth. However, just crossing the parking lot that first morning gave me reason to doubt. Several boy-men who were roughly seven feet tall and sporting patchy beards and pirate-style earrings barked at me as they pulled Marlboros and beef jerky from the pockets of their puffy parkas. (It was, of course, much too warm for such parkas in the first place.) A girl named Danica tugged the plastic barrette out of my hair with one swift motion and pitched it to another girl who crushed it under her knee-high combat boots and laughed. "I've heard of easy targets, but this is fucking *pitiful*," she said, then spat something on the ground that looked like tar. Before I reached the portable door, a semiregular girl wearing a denim skort and a cross around her neck approached me. I sighed with relief and smiled.

"Is anyone home at your house?" she asked.

"Not yet," I said. "My mom just dropped me off."

"Better check anyway," she grinned, flashing her multicolored braces. Then, she punched me hard in each of my small, doughy breasts, shouting triumphantly, "Ding! Dong!" Clearly, I was not prepared for seventh grade.

Jenna sought me out as promised on the parking lot-turned-playground, her Steno pad open with a pencil lodged in the coils, her hair pulled back in a messy bun. She looked older that day and oddly secretarial, like she was getting ready to take shorthand or something. Soon, I will learn that Jenna thinks of clothes as costumes: she always comes dressed as somebody else.

"Shell-shocked?" she asked, leaning beside me on the cyclone fence. I can tell from her tone it isn't really a question.

"I'm not sure this is going to work out," I said. "Maybe I should ask if I can transfer back to sixth grade."

"Do *not* do that!" Jenna exclaimed, tearing into a pack of Skittles with her teeth. "Has your cheese slid completely off the cracker?"

"But we could be in the same grade. We could—"

"You want to trade Christjaener for Hoffman? You want to give up flying under the radar, doing anything you want, for a whole year of nonstop surveillance? We can't even go to the bathroom without a hall pass." Jenna shook the rainbow candies into her mouth and tilted her head back as if planning to gargle. "It's a police state in there, and *we're* not even the delinquents."

Police state? Really? "Where did you go to school before this?"

"I was homeschooled," Jenna said, "but that's completely beside the point."

"So, is your mom a teacher or something?"

"Colleen? Are you kidding? She's a lawyer. Don't get me wrong— she's cool and stylish, and *whip-smart*. But she isn't exactly the motherly type."

"What?" I felt breathless just listening to Jenna, the certainty of her delivery as surprising as the content of her speech. "You call your mother by her first name?"

"Only sometimes," she said, giving her pencil a thoughtful chew. "And mostly just to piss her off."

Within a few weeks, I've been cleared for after-school visits at the Williams house. My mother, a former schoolteacher, is studying to become a bank teller and can use the extra time to herself.

"I know it's a tight squeeze back there," Mr. Williams says, making an apologetic face in the rearview of the family's low-riding Cadillac with the torn-up seats and tinted windows. For a luxury car, it no longer seems so luxurious. Rather, it is dirty and cramped and smells faintly of unwashed dog. "I forgot Jenna was bringing a friend home, so I didn't think to take in the hymnals."

Before I can ask, Jenna explains. She is always good that way—reading people's minds, intercepting their questions, never letting anything linger. "My dad volunteers a lot. He repairs books when they start to fall apart. These are for the Kenney Home."

"That's nice," I smile, and Mr. Williams smiles back, his small, black eyes disappearing into the flesh around the sockets.

"Who wants a Slurpee?" he asks.

"I do! I do!" Mark lurches forward in the passenger seat. His newly spiked hair rises like a rooster's comb just above the headrest.

"What about you girls?"

My mother is watching my weight, and I am watching her watch it, but this isn't something I feel comfortable saying out loud. Instead, "That's OK. I'm still pretty full from lunch."

"I need some CORN NUTS stat, Dad," Jenna says, as he makes a sharp turn into the minimart.

From the glovebox, he withdraws an accordion wallet pleated with bills. "Pump some gas while you're at it," he tells Jenna. "And get me some nachos, Son."

When they are gone on their snack run, I open my math pack and the graph-paper notebook with the light green lines. Mr. Williams' arm stretches the length of the bench seat, and he turns halfway around so he can see what I'm doing. "Algebra?" he asks.

"Pre."

"Are you good at it? Are you good at math? I think Jenna really needs a tutor."

"She seems pretty whip-smart to me," I say, borrowing her word.

"Oh, she's smart," he nods. "No doubt about it. Both my kids are smart, but they're not so much for the standardized tests, you know? They don't show up real bright on the record."

"Were you their teacher?" I ask, glancing at him now. He has turned off the engine but keeps the windows rolled up; soon, a boa of sweat has wrapped around my neck.

"You could call it that," Mr. Williams laughs, letting his fingers dangle over the seat now, a gondolier testing the waters. "I did my best, but sometimes I think my wife's the one with all the brains in the family. Anyway, if you decide you want to earn a few extra bucks, I'd be happy to have you work with Jenna. *Minimal* supervision, I promise." He laughs again and slowly retracts his fingers.

Jenna isn't great with spelling or punctuation, I soon observe, but she is prolific and original, her mind a relentless conveyor belt of ideas. She writes poems and stories and op-ed pieces for a newspaper that doesn't exist, and what she really wants to be when she grows up is a playwright. "Not exactly like Shakespeare," she says. "More like Mamet. I want to make tragedy funny—and cuss a lot in print."

I don't know who this Mamet is, but I can tell our aesthetics don't quite jive. I think comedies should make you laugh, and tragedies should make you cry. I think you should let your audience know what they're in for and not pull some crazy punches at the end.

"I used to want to be a puppeteer," Jenna is explaining to me as we climb the long staircase to her front porch, our hands full of hymnals and foodstuffs. We look like we have robbed a church and moved right on to a movie theater concession stand. "But then I realized I was just being self-conscious about my face, and I shouldn't be, right? I mean, someone has to make the average girls look hot." I think the term for this is self-deprecating humor. "Now I can see myself being writer, actor, and director, but I'll probably start out as a dramaturge."

My head is spinning like those plates in Greek restaurants, except I've never actually been to a Greek restaurant because my mother believes the whole Mediterranean is full of sleazy men with twisty mustaches who only want to pinch and fondle American girls. I have, however, seen those spinning plates in films.

"I don't know what a dramaturge is," I confess, and this is startling, too—the way I have grown accustomed to having the best vocabulary in the room.

"Don't worry," Jenna says, kicking the front door open with the heel of her rain-stained cowboy boots. "I'll fill you in on everything."

Everything, in this case, means a national competition called Odyssey of the Mind that Jenna is hell-bent on entering. "I want to get Liann and Mindy and some of the other girls from my grade to do it, and since you're technically supposed to be in sixth grade anyway, you can compete with us. It's going to be a blast."

"And what is it exactly?"

"All in good time," she promises, dumping the hymnals on the dining room table and leading me into the kitchen. "What do you want to drink?"

"I'm fine with water," I say.

"That's ridiculous. Nobody's fine with water. Have a soda," she says, "or some Tang or something. Mark! Will you go feed Beau and the rabbits?"

"You have rabbits?"

"We used to have more, but we're down to sixteen, give or take. Straw?" She holds out a bag of fifty bendy straws, and I take one just to be polite.

"Where are they—your rabbits?"

"In the backyard," Jenna says, gesturing toward the window. "We have to keep them in hutches, of course, or the dog will lose his mind." She takes a soup spoon to a jar of peanut butter, makes a decadent scoop, then holds the spoon in her mouth as she leads me up another set of stairs. This time, there is a rickety white banister, and the ceiling seems to close in around us as we ascend. "Old houses," Jenna mutters, the peanut butter still gluey between her lips, the spoon clanging to the floor. I notice with some amazement that she never goes back to pick it up. "But do you know what is so frickin' awesome about this place? It's over one hundred years old, and every spring we're featured on the Historic Homes Tour!"

If my mom had been there—which, thankfully, she wasn't—I'm pretty sure she would have described Jenna's room as "squalid," "putrid," probably a "hovel," since my mother was especially fond of condemning nouns. But Jenna called the room her "garret," which suited her perfectly as an artist, she said. She twirled around the effusing hamper, then stripped down to her skivvies and went searching through the bed sheets for her sweats.

"See that house out there, the big colonial on the other side of the tennis courts?" Jenna unhooked her bra, which was my intuitive cue to look away.

I perched on the window seat, the wrappers of several Mars bars crinkling beneath me. "I think so," I said, but really all I saw were the hemlocks and live oaks, steadfast as ever, with their leaves that never changed.

"That is Matthew McDaniel's house. He goes to Blanchet and lettered last year in cross-country and crew. And if it seems like I know everything about him," Jenna said, standing on the window seat now and tying back the curtains with two washcloths, "it's because I do. I fully intend to marry him in ten years, and he will most definitely be taking me to my senior prom well before then."

I nodded. I wasn't sure what to say. Jenna didn't speak in suppositions. For her, saying something seemed to make it true.

"OK, so, let's get down to business." She was wearing one pink sock and one green, but this may have been on purpose. She opened the bag of CORN NUTS and began to glide around her room. "I'm really into this idea of postmodern theater. Does that mean anything to you?"

I shrugged. "Not really. I know I like musicals, and I'm partial to a good British farce."

Jenna shot me with one of her scrunchies. "Get serious, Julie! That's so passé. We're never going to win Odyssey of the Mind with something textbook. Do you know about breaking the fourth wall?"

I wanted to come up with a clever response, but instead I opened my Coke and dug around in my book bag for the straw.

"Basically, it's when you're watching a show, and the characters seem at first only to be talking to each other. Then, suddenly, they start talking to *you*, the person in the audience. They step out of character to deliver a message or reveal something about the script. Breaking the fourth wall is the moment when a production goes meta."

"So—just to make sure I'm following—you want to enter this play competition—"

Jenna leapt to her feet and rummaged through her desk until she found a colorful brochure, which she promptly thrust into my hands. "Not a *play* competition exactly. Odyssey of the Mind is an exercise in problem-solving through performance. I want to play with the idea of walls and breaking them down. We could make a bunch of bricks out of papier-mâché and stack them into walls of varying heights. But then I was trying to figure out about the historical component. The judges like there to be something with math or social studies or literature, and then it hit me—THE BERLIN WALL!" She was as animated as I had ever seen her, and her cheeks glowed as red as the star on a San Pellegrino bottle. I had just tripped over one on the floor. "And you know how people were taking pieces of it home and selling pieces of it, and they're only just now really saying that they've finished dismantling it?" I nodded again, but to be honest, I hadn't been keeping up with the news.

"Oh my god, Julie! Oh my god!" Jenna flung open the double doors to her closet. She had the kind of crystal door knobs that I liked. "I think I have a Ronald Reagan mask! And if it's not in here, it'll be in Mark's room. I wore it for Halloween a couple years ago. Don't you remember—when he was saying to Gorbachev, 'Tear down this wall!' Well, I could say that, and we could have pickaxes and wheelbarrows on stage, and—" Jenna lunged toward me, feverish with joy, and swept my neatly curled bangs from my forehead. "Do you think you could wear a flesh-toned bathing cap? Would you mind? I *know* my mother has one because she hates to get her hair wet, and then"—she twirled around again, eyes alighting on the multipack of markers on her desk—"we'll draw that big, goofy birthmark on your scalp!"

Mrs. Williams was supposed to drive me home that night, but she got tied up with a court case and called to say she wouldn't get in till late. "It happens a lot," Jenna said with a wave of her hand. "She's a litigator, so it comes with the territory."

"Well, do you think your dad could take me home?" I asked.

"No, he's busy." Her voice was firm, definitive as ever. "But you can use my phone to call your parents," she offered, pointing to the bedside table.

"There's a phone in here?" Mark had wandered in before with the cordless.

"We have two lines," she replied. "See those lips?" They looked just like the mouth on the old Twizzlers commercials. I thought they were for decoration. "Pick up the top one and dial."

By the time my dad arrived, it was dark outside and raining. He motioned for me to hop in the front seat, even though my mother's rule book clearly stated I was to ride in the back until high school.

"Did you have fun?" he asked, patting my knee and turning down the Barry Manilow.

"I think so. Yeah—I mean—Jenna is fun. She's just—I don't know—kind of exhausting."

"Well, touché!" he laughed, which surprised me since the word is French, and my father is famously stumped when it comes to other languages. "I'd be willing to bet big money that's how a lot of your friends around the neighborhood feel after playing with *you*."

"Yeah, that's probably true." I returned his laugh with a little giggle of my own.

"So, tell me," my father said, in that stage-whisper way he had of trying to sound casual. "What's it like in there?"

"At the Williams'?"

He nodded, his eyes fixed on the road as the windshield wipers sloshed back and forth across the glass.

"It's nice—*old*. Did you know their house is on the Historic Homes Tour?"

"I guess what I'm getting at is—Mr. Williams—he really doesn't work at all?"

"Well . . ." I groped around in my mind for the right words to answer. "He does a lot of volunteer work, repairs old books. And you know, he used to homeschool Jenna and Mark."

"I don't know," my father sighed. "Doesn't feel right, this whole stay-at-home husband business. I think a man should support his family—and a woman should be at home with her kids."

"But Mrs. Williams is a litigator," I protest. "That's a very important kind of lawyer."

"Well, if she wanted to be a litigator so bad, maybe she shouldn't have had a family," he replied.

"You want *me* to have an important job someday—*and* a family," I shot back, my voice coming swift and strong as Jenna's.

"Of course, Smidge. Women have to have their own work to fall back on. But we know you'll do the right thing and put your job on hold when your kids are small, the same way your mother did for you."

A cold feeling began to slither down my back. I was damp from the rain, but it wasn't that. It was something internal, hard to explain. I thought about the plaque on my bedroom door, the one designed for me before I was even born—back when I was just an idea of a person. In flourished script, the plaque read *Julie Marie Wade, Attorney-at-Law.*

"But what if Mr. Williams was the litigator? Would he have to put that job on hold when his kids were small?" I studied my father's jawline by the headlights of passing cars.

"Well, that's just it," he sighed. "Mr. Williams *isn't*."

Now whenever we see the Williamses at church, I contort like an awkward sea creature, knowing my parents have no interest in befriending Jenna's parents, that, in fact, they seem to think poorly of them ("their priorities are way out of whack!"), and I fear their judgments will show. My mother has remarked to my father on more than one occasion: "If we have to buy *your* clothes at the Big & Tall Shop, where in Heaven's name does Colleen buy Dan's clothes—West Seattle Tent & Awning?" My father has remarked to my mother, also within my earshot: "Maybe Colleen doesn't buy Dan's clothes. Maybe he has to buy them for himself." My mother's reply, predictable as always: "Right. With *her* money."

Another time, when he thought I had gone downstairs, I heard my father ask my mother, "What's a classy, petite gal like that doing with such a big slob anyway? Makes you wonder if she's getting some on the side."

The fact was, I only recognized this euphemism because Jenna had used it to relay one of her many conspiracy theories. "Pastor Winterstein has something going on the side with Miss Christjaener. I *guarantee* it." She was impersonating George Zimmer from the Men's Wearhouse commercials, pointing her finger and underlining things in the air.

"You don't know that," I said. "He's married to Boots, the organist, and they've been together for like a hundred years."

"Variety," Jenna replied, nonplussed. "Men *can't* be monogamous. It's not in their DNA." As with everything else, she left no room for argument.

This particular Sunday was memorable because of one of Pastor Winterstein's prayers. He led us first through the usual rote recitations of gratitude and penitence, and then, as always, opened space for others to offer their prayers. People prayed for sick relatives, for lost jobs, for children who had been sent back to juvie. Sometimes they tried to be more abstract, more coded about their troubles. It was common to hear, "For the compassion to turn the other cheek" or "For strength in the face of temptation." But then Pastor Winterstein's deep, velvety voice rejoined the series of spoken offerings: "Father, we pray on behalf of all the women in our congregation who have received harassing phone calls. Please give them comfort, and please let these obscenities cease."

Jenna and I exchanged glances, as we always did. Her eyes were impishly blue. She pointed to Pastor Winterstein and then to Miss Christjaener, sitting alone in the first row, dressed always in black like she had come for a funeral. Jenna made a circle with her thumb and forefinger and then the gesture for intercourse she had taught me proudly. I rolled my eyes but giggled a little in spite of myself. That's when my mother pressed down hard on my foot with her heel.

"May I please go to Jenna's house after church today?" I implore my parents during the recessional song.

"Is your homework done?"

"Yes—and impeccably."

"Don't push it," my mother snaps. Her tone matches her faux alligator clutch purse.

"It's just that we have the Odyssey of the Mind tournament coming up, and there's the soundtrack we have to finish making, and—"

"This better be something you can put on your high school applications, that's all I can say," she sighs. I take off to find Jenna before she can come up with a reason to stop me.

"I want to work Humpty-Dumpty into it somehow," Jenna says. "And Rapunzel, too, because it's a high castle wall the prince has to climb before he gets to her hair. History is good, but myths are better. The postmodernists love them because they're stories that don't have to make sense."

"What is this project you're working on?" Mrs. Williams wants to know. We are riding home from church in her snazzy red sedan, but even though the car is hers, Mr. Williams is driving.

"It's a performance piece about breaking down walls," Jenna begins. "We're interested in everything having to do with walls. Mindy is going to make actual balloon-flowers on stage during the show and attach them to the walls."

"Very nice," Mrs. Williams smiles. "I like it. Wallflowers."

"*Exactly.* Later, Liann is going to ride through on a little girl's bike with training wheels and pop all of them with a pin."

"Interesting," she nods. "I can see this is going to be very dynamic."

"It's going to be more than dynamic," Jenna exclaims. "It's going to be *dynamite!*"

"Let me know if you want to borrow *The Wall*," Mrs. Williams offers, running her hands through her Diane Keaton hair. "I have it on record and cassette."

"Genius, Colleen!" Jenna says. "Pure genius."

"What's *The Wall?*"

Jenna's and Mrs. Williams' heads swivel toward me simultaneously, and then they exclaim in unison, as if they had planned it that way: "Pink Floyd!"

When we get inside the house, Mr. Williams disappears down the basement stairs, just as he always does, and Mrs. Williams immediately takes off her shoes. My mother doesn't believe in walking around barefoot, which is why you'll find a pair of ratty Dearfoams slippers in almost any room of our house. But Mrs. Williams has perfect, pedicured toes, which she wiggles happily on the living room rug, then asks Jenna to pour her a glass of Franzia from the fridge.

"I have a brief to work on, Jenna," she says, "so here's twenty dollars. Why don't you girls order a pizza? Mark's gone over to Tyler's house, and I'm sure your father can fend for himself."

"Cool. Thanks." Jenna is barefoot now, too, and when she sees me looking at her feet, she laughs and says, "You know you can take your shoes off if you want. Mark and I finally did our chores, so the floors and rugs are clean—for the moment."

I leave my loafers in first position by the door.

"So, what kind of pizza do you like?" Jenna asks, carrying a magnet into the dining room that has the Domino's phone number printed on top of a large slice of pepperoni.

"Any kind—*all* kinds," I stutter.

"Julie, what's going on? I can read you like a book, and this question isn't that hard."

I glance at Mrs. Williams reclining on the white couch, her violet toenails without a chip or smudge, the glass of wine in her hand. "I'm just—I've never—we don't—"

"Out with it!" Jenna demands.

"I've never had pizza delivered before."

Now Mrs. Williams looks up from her leather folder and furrows her brow. "Do your parents prefer carryout?" she asks.

"No, I mean, I've only ever had pizza at school—and from my grocer's freezer." I try to make a joke, but Jenna and her mother have identical expressions on their faces. Mrs. Williams is pale, and Jenna is rubicund—another word I have learned from her—but they seem to regard me the way people must have regarded Columbus when he suggested the whole flat-earth story was just a myth.

"*Never?*" Their voices, synchronized again.

I shake my head. "No. My mother doesn't believe in people delivering things to your house."

Mrs. Williams reaches for her wine glass first, then cocks her head. "And why is that exactly?"

"Well, she thinks that, for instance, if you order a pizza and somebody who is working for five dollars an hour plus tips sees that you live in a really nice house, they'll tell all their friends, and when their shift is over, they'll come back and rob you. If you're still home or if you put up a fight, they might even kill you."

I have probably said too much, but Jenna and her mother begin to howl with laughter.

They laugh so hard that Mr. Williams lumbers up the basement stairs and calls from the kitchen, "What's so funny?"

Jenna grins at me. "You're *plangent*, that's what you are. That's why we were meant to be friends. Maybe we should be writing a performance piece about your mother."

Mrs. Williams wipes her eyes with a tissue and instructs us to order bread sticks and chicken wings, too. "She needs to have the whole experience," Mrs. Williams says.

While Jenna is placing the call, I take a seat on one of the brocade, wingback chairs near the fireplace. "I don't know how *anyone* could raise children without Domino's," Mrs. Williams sighs. She seems to be speaking mostly to herself. "They're a godsend."

Later, in Jenna's bedroom, we share the window seat and scarf down the pizza and sides. "And you've never had Chinese takeout before either?" she asks, stunned.

"Just to settle the matter once and for all," I say, mimicking my friend's dramatic flair, "*never,* in my *entire* life, has *anyone* come to my door with food and given it to me in exchange for money."

Jenna gapes at me and mimes tears before breaking into boisterous laughter.

Then, just as suddenly: "Is my dad paying you to be my friend?" There is no segue to indicate that we are switching gears, but then with Jenna, there is never a segue. My mouth drops open, a drawbridge of surprise.

"I know—" she says, interrupting me before I can even assemble the words "—he wouldn't phrase it that way. He'd ask you to be my tutor because I don't get the best grades, but really, I think it's so I won't be alone, just daydreaming all the time. My friend-making skills might be even worse than my grades."

"Jenna," I say, "you're my friend because I like you. You're fun to be around. No one is paying me to spend time here."

"But he asked you, didn't he?" She has started wandering around the room, her MO, but this time while tugging on the sticky strings of a Koosh ball.

"Does it really matter?"

"Only to the extent that you're not on the Dad tab," Jenna replies. "Because it turns out my last three friends were all getting paid to spend time with me, and I guess the funds must have dried up when my schoolwork didn't improve because I never heard from any of them again." She puts on her magician's hat for effect. "Poof! Gone."

"That won't happen with me," I say, twisting her wand till it turns into flowers. "We've got a play to put on."

"Uh—"

"I *mean,* an exercise in performative problem-solving!"

Remember when I told you this story doesn't end well? I should have said that I'm sorry, and if it were up to me, I'd change it, but I can't. The truth is, I didn't even see it coming.

Maybe there were signs. Maybe I should have thought it strange that Sunday night when Mrs. Williams told Jenna to ask her father to take me home, and Jenna insisted that her mother do it. She said she was up to her earlobes in work, and Mr. Williams had nothing to do but fix old books and play video games.

"No," Jenna said, stomping her foot the way a child might, but unwavering at the same time like a schoolmarm. "You do it."

On the car ride, I told Mrs. Williams about the *Julie Marie Wade, Attorney-at-Law* plaque on my bedroom door. "My parents had it made because they wanted to remind me of my potential, even before I could read. They wanted me to grow up knowing I could succeed in any professional career, even if I didn't do it forever."

"I can see that," Mrs. Wiliams mused, "but it does feel like a lot of pressure for a kid to come home to a law office every night."

I asked her if she ever felt like she had to choose between being a good lawyer and being a good mom.

"*Choose,* no—but *compromise,* yes." She selected her words very carefully, the way lawyers always did on TV. "That's true for everyone, though, I think. Not just for working mothers."

We didn't place at Odyssey of the Mind, and Jenna was distraught for months afterwards. The judges noted that we were an "enthusiastic ensemble" but thought we "tried to take on too much" and "our objectives were muddled." The last-minute addition of Frost's "Mending Wall," which I read from behind a curtain like the disembodied voice of the Wizard of Oz, might have seemed gimmicky to the crowd, but all of us really loved the poem.

Jenna went to horseback-riding camp over the summer, which she always did, and then we found each other again in Christjaener's class: me in eighth grade, Jenna in seventh. Miss Hoffman returned to school as Mrs. Weatherhogg, having married the man who drove the local flower truck and become de facto mom to his three children. She also joined the growing roster of victims of the Calvary Lutheran obscene phone caller, who apparently panted a lot and told the women in great detail about outfits he had seen them wear. Everyone assumed it was one of the junior high delinquents.

Jenna told me that all she wanted for Christmas was a Thigh-Master because she had decided to tone up to form a space at the top of her legs, a gap where the thighs didn't touch. "I want enough room for a keyhole's worth of light to pass through," she said.

My mother had recently bought us a ThighMaster to share, and I told Jenna she could use it whenever she came over.

We were Nairing our legs at the time, something I had never attempted before, but Jenna said it was better to burn off the hair than try to get it all with a razor. I wasn't even supposed to be shaving.

"Why do you have a ThighMaster anyway?" she asked, as we sat on the lip of the grimy tub, our pant legs rolled up, waiting for the timer to ding.

"My mom thought I was going to be tall and skinny like Gwyneth Paltrow." I paused for effect, the way Jenna taught me. The power of a line was in its delivery. "She has never quite recovered from the disappointment."

Jenna grabbed my wrist, as if she was bracing herself for a blow. "Are you kidding me? You *are* tall and skinny!"

"Well, I'm *tall*," I told her, "but so are you."

"I'm tall like a wall," Jenna said. "You're tall like a statue."

"What does that mean?" I had never looked at her across this line before.

"It means you're well-sculpted. You have curves in all the right places. You're on your way, Leading Lady." Jenna raised an imaginary champagne flute and pretended to toast. "Even my father thinks so."

"What?" The timer dinged, and she tossed me a towel. "Everyone thinks I should be more like you."

Another time, watching Matthew McDaniel's house through our binoculars, Jenna asked me if I wanted to be a virgin when I got married.

"I'm not sure I'm going to marry actually," I said. "And I'd rather not die a virgin if I can help it."

"You won't have any problem there," she replied, her voice so much softer now than it used to be, and flatter, too—a murmury monotone.

"Did you give up inflection for Lent or something?" I teased, but Jenna didn't seem to get the joke.

"It doesn't matter if I have sex before marriage or not," she said. "Girls who ride horses as much as I do get their hymens broken early."

"But—you can still be a virgin without a hymen, right?"

Jenna held a piece of celery between her teeth like a cigar. She mock-exhaled, then did her best George Burns: "You *can* be, honey, but really, what's the point?"

The last evening I ever spent with Jenna, her mother came home early, happy to have won a case. Strangely, though, she didn't bother to tell Jenna's father, even to call down to him from the top of the basement stairs.

"I brought Chinese food to celebrate!" she proclaimed, a late twentieth-century prophet in her power suit and pearls. "Lo mein. Fried rice. Wontons. The works! Mark, do me a favor and run down and get the food from the car."

"Well done, Colleen," Jenna nodded her approval over a glass of Crystal Light.

The heels skittered across the floor, the briefcase rested on the counter, the wine poured forth from the fridge, and Mrs. Williams told me I should stay for dinner. "I'm in the mood for a girls' night.

Let's watch a movie," she said. "What about *Manhattan* or *Hannah and Her Sisters*?" She looked at me. "Any preference?"

I shook my head. "I don't know those movies," I said.

"You don't know *Manhattan*?" Jenna threw her hands in the air and rushed to the video cabinet. "What about *Annie Hall*? You *have* to know Annie Hall!"

"Oh, they're Woody Allen movies," I sighed. "My mother doesn't—isn't—a fan."

"He's our favorite," Jenna said, laying out the VHS tapes with all the ceremony of communion wafers and sacramental wine.

"What is it she objects to about the movies?" Mrs. Williams asked, motioning for Mark to bring the food directly into the living room.

"I think it's more about him than his movies," I replied. Mrs. Williams slid the chopsticks out of their paper sheath and nodded for me to continue. I liked how she moved them about as if conducting a musical score. "It's just that whole thing about how he married his daughter. I know she was adopted and all, but it really creeped my mother out."

"You know what really creeps me out?" Jenna asked, sitting back on her heels. I could tell from her tone it wasn't really a question. "All-girls, Catholic schools."

About an hour before, I had confided in Jenna that my mother was sending me to Holy Names Academy in the fall. They offered merit-based scholarships, and their graduates were guaranteed to go on to do great things. I even tried a George Zimmer impersonation when I broke the news.

"Why is that?" Mrs. Williams laughed, bemused, guiding a fried dumpling deftly to her mouth.

"They're full of lesbians," Jenna said, deadpan. "Some come in gay, but everybody leaves that way."

I don't know much about theater—not really. Jenna and I used to talk about hosting our own variety show, the celebrities we'd get to make cameos, and the role of improvisation in sketch comedy. We also marveled often and aloud at how Vicki Lawrence managed to transform herself so completely into Mama. She made you forget she was really just a young woman in a gray wig and a floral dress with nylons socks that sagged below her knees. I laughed because she reminded me of the Lutherans.

In our Odyssey of the Mind production, Jenna wanted to use walls as dividers so people in the audience could see what was happening simultaneously at the same moment in history or in the same house even. But the meaning of the walls kept changing, which I have to admit in retrospect made our performance especially hard to follow.

When I was in high school, a story came out in all the local papers that a West Seattle man had sexually assaulted a number of young girls, all of whom had been about his daughter's age. Reports never confirmed whether the daughter herself had been subject to abuse or if she might have suspected her father. In the course of this trial, during which he was sentenced to thirteen years in the state penitentiary, it was further revealed that the same man had been responsible for several years of obscene phone calls to female members of the congregation at Calvary Lutheran Church.

My parents left Calvary once rumors about the Williamses surfaced and soon rejoined their old flock at St. Paul's. Fourteen blocks was just far enough to make a fresh start in West Seattle after all, and a fresh start could last my mother at least a few years.

Jenna never returned any of my calls, of course, which made more sense after the news story broke but was still never easy for me to accept. The church secretary at Calvary told my mother it was Mrs. Williams who caught her husband on the telephone, walked in to find him "compromised" on their bed, telling someone's teenage daughter that he wanted her to strip slowly for him. And from this, a much larger unraveling began—as terrifying and convoluted as any myth, or any truth.

Much later, my mother would call me in my grown-up apartment and ask, her voice gravelly with fear, "Did Dan Williams do something to you? Is that why you're"—she stammered still, months after my coming out—"the way you are?"

"No, Mom," I said, deadpan. "It was Catholic school. It turned me so gay. If you hadn't sent me there, I'd have a husband and three kids by now."

Though I am not a playwright and never will be, I can picture a dim stage with a series of spotlighted partitions. In one stall, two thirteen-year-old girls sprawl on a cluttered bed listening to *The Wall* and bicycling their newly Naired legs. In another, a woman in her forties, who bears a striking resemblance to Diane Keaton, takes notes on a yellow legal pad for an upcoming trial. In the last stall, we find a large man alone in a basement, reclining in a La-Z-Boy. He has a phone in his lap, the kind where the push-button numbers line the receiver, and the receiver lights up in the dark. There is a book, too, folded along its stapled seam—a directory of some kind. We can't make out his face, and across the wall, we see the silhouette of a little boy, his newly spiked hair rising like a rooster's comb.

But even this is too much to look at. Anything more, and we, the audience, the witnesses, would implode.

ACKNOWLEDGMENTS

Thank you to the Barbara Deming Memorial Fund for their valuable support of *Other People's Mothers* as this project was first beginning to take shape.

Thank you to Stephanye Hunter for believing in my work and to the entire team at University Press of Florida for bringing my book to beautiful fruition.

I am forever grateful to my mentors—Dana Anderson, Tom Campbell, Susanne Paola Antonetta, Bruce Beasley, Brenda Miller, Annette Allen (rest in poetry), and Catherine Fosl—for their insight and generosity, and to my enduring friends—Anna Rhodes, James Allen Hall, Denise Duhamel, John Dufresne, Debra Dean, and Cindy Chinelly—who have always welcomed my stories and regaled me with their own.

Thank you to Paul Griner for his early feedback on some of the work included here.

Thank you to all the nonmothers, especially Linda Ann Wade and Kathe Curran, who modeled for me another path.

Thank you to my colleagues and students at Florida International University, where my writing and teaching life has flourished these past thirteen years.

Special gratitude to Kim Striegel, the best mother I know, for her enthusiasm for this book, and to all my "Outlaws"—Kim, Matt, Evie, Nolan "Super Hondo," and Sam—for welcoming me into their lives long before the law recognized us as family.

Greenies to Tina and Beaufort, who lounged on my computer and purred in my lap as I wrote, revised, and submitted these pages.

And always, to Angie Griffin, my first reader and favorite person, my synonym for home.

Literary Acknowledgments

Thank you to the editors of the following publications where these chapters, often in altered form, first appeared:

"Mrs. Mann [Or a Study of the Fates of Different Drummers]," *Bayou*, 2015.

"Mrs. Lennox [Or a Study of Change as Crisis or Caricature]," *ROAR Magazine*, 2013.

"Mrs. Newport [Or a Study of Jealousy as a Blue-Eyed Monster]," *Lalitamba*, 2015.

"Mrs. Arlington [Or a Study of Apocalypse as an After-School Special]," *Passages North*, 2012.

"Mrs. Bigelow [Or a Study of Death as the Last Bouquet]," *Harpur Palate*, 2012. Finalist for the *Harpur Palate* Creative Nonfiction Prize.

"Mrs. Magnussen [Or a Study of Desire That Doesn't Cover All the Bases]," *Oyez Review*, 2014.

"Mrs. Williams [Or a Study of Postmodernism and the Many Ways That Walls Are Broken]," *Cincinnati Review*, 2024.

Nota bene: *Other People's Mothers* is an honest account of my coming of age. As with all literary translations of lived experience, memory and craft have been mobilized in service of story. The names of parents and children in this collection have been changed out of respect for their privacy.

Julie Marie Wade was born in Seattle in 1979. She completed a Master of Arts in English at Western Washington University, a Master of Fine Arts in poetry at the University of Pittsburgh, and a PhD in interdisciplinary humanities with a creative nonfiction dissertation at the University of Louisville. She is the author of many collections of poetry, prose, and hybrid forms, including most recently *Otherwise: Essays; Quick Change Artist: Poems; Fisk, by Analogy;* and *The Latest: 20 Ghazals for 2020,* co-authored with Denise Duhamel. A finalist for the National Poetry Series and a winner of the Lambda Literary Award for Lesbian Memoir, Wade is professor of English and creative writing at Florida International University in Miami and makes her home with Angie Griffin and their two cats in Dania Beach.